K

How to Write about the Social Sciences

How to Write about the Social Sciences

LEE CUBA
Wellesley College

JOHN COCKING
University of East London

 LONGMAN

Addison Wesley Longman Limited
Edinburgh Gate, Harlow
Essex CM20 2JE, England
and Associated Companies throughout the world

A short Guide to Writing about Social Science, 2nd Edition, copyright © 1993 by
Lee Cuba

This edition first published in 1994 by
HarperCollins College Division
This edition published in 1997
by Addison Wesley Longman

John Cocking asserts the moral right to be identified as the author of the adapted
material.

British Library Cataloguing in Publication Data
A catalogue record for this book is available from the British Library.

ISBN 0-582-32578-1

Produced through Longman Malaysia, PP

Contents

Acknowledgements (UK Edition)

In adapting this text I have drawn upon my experience of teaching and learning at the University of East London and I am very grateful for all the opportunities, over a number of years, for learning and reflection with students and colleagues. In particular, I have learned much from Audrey Joyce whose commitment to, and understanding of, effective teaching in higher education provides a model of the 'good practitioner'.

The book itself has benefited from the critical observations of David Holmes, Nancy Kelly and Elaine Pullen, and I am indebted to Penny Read for her expertise and specialist knowledge of library and information systems and without whom the wholly revised Chapter Two would have been impossible.

I am very grateful to Jacqueline Owusu for typing the different drafts with such patience, skill and good humour and to Gita Gopalgii for her co-ordinating role.

Finally, I wish to thank Ben for his contribution to Chapter Four, for his calm and perception and for never letting me forget how students really tackle their writing tasks!

John Cocking

1. The Process of Writing

Social scientists write about the methods they use to collect and analyse social data, and about the results these methods yield. They rarely examine the process of writing itself (with some notable exceptions, for example Becker (1986) and Mills (1970)). If you are to negotiate successfully your undergraduate studies, you will need to become a confident and effective writer.

PROCESS AND PRACTICE

Writing involves the development and application of a range of skills and competencies which form over a period of time. To become an effective writer therefore requires a **great deal of practice in writing, editing and re-writing** – in sharpening words and phrases so that ideas and concepts are more clearly expressed. In this sense, the old adage, practice makes perfect has some relevance. But writing is more than this. It involves a set of routines which develop around and help shape the activity or practice of writing. To become an effective writer, you must understand **how** you write. You must be aware of the routines you follow and the characteristics of your overall approach.

DIRECTION AND APPROACH

Your approach to your writing will be influenced by your understanding of what is involved. If you are uncertain or misguided, problems will emerge. For example, many undergraduate students believe that essay writing is a task which involves a strict sequence of events. First a topic is chosen (or, more probably, it is assigned), a bibliography is compiled, data are collected, notes are taken and organised and then, when all these things have been completed, **writing begins**.

This is a total misconception of the process of writing. Firstly, it fails to give sufficient importance to 'creativity'. The irony of seeing writing as the grand conclusion to weeks of research is that it serves as a deterrent to writing in the first place. Attempting to 'know' everything before beginning to write can create a 'writer's block' of seemingly insurmountable proportions. Students who follow this approach frequently put off writing until the essay is fully outlined and researched; they tend to prevaricate on the grounds that they 'don't know enough' and continue to collect more information and data. As the hand-in date for the essay approaches, problems of writing become problems of time, that is, there isn't enough!

To define writing as simply communicating ideas to others ignores the fact that when we write we communicate something of ourselves. When we write an essay, a paragraph or even a sentence, we 'objectify' our thoughts, i.e. we separate them from ourselves and they assume an existence and a nature of their own. For example, have you ever re-read something you have previously written, perhaps an essay you wrote before going to university or a diary entry of some months ago? If you have, you may have been surprised that you were reading something written by yourself – 'Was it **really me** who wrote this!' (If you haven't experienced this, try it out.) In re-reading your previous work, you are forced to confront and experience the objective reality of your words.

Of course, months or years need not elapse before we come to see our writing as distinct from ourselves. The moment we write a sentence we may realise that it doesn't express what we originally had in mind. We might write, 'there are two reasons why . . .', and realise suddenly that there are three reasons – or that one of our two reasons isn't much of a reason after all and can be omitted.

This view of writing provides a continuous opportunity to deepen our understanding, to be more thoughtful and insightful. For this reason, it is important to think about writing as a process – not wholly as an outcome – in which the activity of writing is followed by individual reflection, review and re-writing. In other words, writing is an analytical and creative project.

At the same time writing is not an open, never-ending activity. It does of course conclude; after all, your tutor really wants to see that essay you have been working on. But it is important to understand the process in which you are engaged and the necessity for returning to your drafts to consider and assess how they can be developed and improved. This recursive activity is represented in the diagram below:

FIGURE 1.

Masiello 1993

In following the approach of the above diagram you will find it useful to discuss matters with your fellow students, especially at the 'invention' and 'brainstorming' stages, and with your tutor at the 'early drafting' and 'middle drafting' stages. At an early stage, it is useful to establish with your tutor the appropriateness of the direction and parameters of your writing so that you can proceed to develop and organise your assignment in greater depth. By the middle draft stage you should have developed your ideas sufficiently and be concerned with the general question of coherence, i.e. does the essay hang together, are the different paragraphs linked, and appropriate transitional phrases and words in place?

Furthermore, you will need to give close attention to the final stages of your assignment and consider how it is to conclude. Again, it is useful to discuss these matters with your peers and your tutor. Finally, you will need to evaluate critically and edit your draft, while at the same time giving thought to the technical aspects to ensure high standards of presentation.

Throughout your writing, you should critically review your work. As you reflect on what you have written, new ideas will emerge and new ways of organising and developing your argument will become evident and necessary. Becoming more accomplished in these processes will not only help to re-shape and improve your writing, but will also enhance your learning at a deeper and more substantive level in your specialist area of study.

ESTABLISHING A WRITING STRATEGY

Your first draft cannot – should not – be your final product. This approach to writing has many advantages. Most importantly, it frees you from the burden of developing a tightly-knit argument **before** committing your thoughts to paper. Knowing what you want to say becomes clearer **after** your writing task begins, and you will find that the ideas you wish to discuss and the contents you wish to include in your assignment will become clearer during the process of **re-writing**. In establishing a writing strategy you should think about the following:

• **flexibility** – be willing to part with your words where necessary. Remember, there are many ways to express your ideas; being attached to a particular form of words not only ignores the emergent nature of your writing style, but it deflects your understanding of what you are trying to write about.

- **feedback** – seek feedback from others, especially your tutors and other students. Learn to deal with constructive criticism of your writing. Never regard criticism of your work as a personal attack on your intellectual capabilities and/or your writing ability. Of course you would welcome a little praise for your writing, but examining the constructive criticism of others gives you an additional chance to 'get it right'. Viewing your words objectively, as separate from yourself, is a necessary condition to accepting and benefiting from the views of others.
- **peer support** – take advantage of your contact with fellow students and **learn to learn from them**. Offer to read and provide feedback on their writing. This will help you to gain confidence and to develop critical editorial and evaluative skills which you can apply to your own work.

Remember that readers can only assess the contents and arguments as they appear in a piece of writing. They cannot be expected to know and fully appreciate the unstated information and understanding – the thinking, planning, researching, writing and rewriting – which has preceded your efforts. Learning to distance yourself from your own writing is an essential first step in learning to accept criticism, and in acquiring the skills of self-editing, and thereby beginning to evolve an effective writing strategy.

Writing, reflecting and re-writing: an example

The best way to discover how editing and re-writing can improve the quality of your work is to trace their effects through a series of drafts. The following example shows how one writer has attempted to improve his writing through reflection and re-writing.

Draft 1

> Learning to talk 'like an Alaskan' is an important part of becoming an Alaskan. It is one's claim to membership, part of the frontier experience. Noticeably, residents of Anchorage

do not refer to themselves as 'Anchoragites' but as 'Alaskans.' Identification with the state rather than the city is strong, an obvious point to those who have seen the sprawl of urban Anchorage. Thus, the majority of the words unique to Alaska are descriptive of the region, rather than the city itself. Examples include: outside; cheechako; sourdough; cabin fever. Many others have something to do with the weather. Placing bets on the date of 'freeze up' and 'break up' are annual events, as is speculation over when the 'termination dust' (first snow of the season) will arrive. 'White out' is not something a secretary uses but it is a hazardous condition caused by 'ice fog' on which light reflects off the snow yet casts no shadow. A 'cache' used to be a place where food was stored out of reach of wild animals; today it refers to a business and is often preceded by the appropriate product name, as in the book cache, the stamp and coin cache. Though many of the cruder elements of early Alaska have vanished from the streets of downtown Anchorage, the region's frontier history lives on in daily conversation.

Author's note

The paragraph is weak in at least three ways:

- It is plagued with imprecise language. For example the first sentence '. . . is an important part of becoming an Alaskan . . .' What does this mean?
- It assumes that readers have good background information about the topic. Failure to define 'outside', 'cheechako', 'sourdough' and 'cabin fever' weakens the claim that contemporary Alaskan dialogue is grounded in the imagery of its frontier history.
- There is too much material for inclusion in one paragraph. The first part of the paragraph focuses on how Alaskans use a frontier vocabulary to distinguish themselves from others, while many of the examples at the end of the passage deal with the importance of climate to early Alaskan life.

Draft II

Learning to talk 'like an Alaskan' is a first step for new
arrivals to Alaska. It is one's claim to membership, an
integral part of the frontier experience. Noticeably, residents
of Anchorage do not refer to themselves as 'Anchoragites'
but as 'Alaskans.' Identification with the state rather than
with the city is strong for reasons obvious to those who
have seen the urban sprawl of Anchorage. Thus, the
majority of the words unique to Alaska are descriptive
of the region, rather than of the city itself. Most frequently
heard is the term 'outside', which refers to any place
which is not Alaska. Newcomers are called 'cheechakos'
and old-timers 'sourdoughs,' both linguistic vestiges
from the days of the Alaska gold rush. The former is
derivative of 'Chicago' and connotes the inexperience
often displayed by newcomers to Alaska. A sourdough,
on the other hand, was a veteran prospector, the name
coming from the type of bread carried on the trail. Several
other such characterisations have their origin in earlier times
when climate played a major role in affecting the course of
Alaskan life. The restless claustrophobic feeling which
accompanies the long hours of winter darkness is familiarly
known as 'cabin fever.'

Placing bets on the dates of 'freeze up' and 'break up' are
annual events, as is speculation over when the 'termination
dust' (first snow of the season) will arrive. 'White out' is not
an office supply but a hazardous condition caused by 'ice fog'
in which light reflects off the snow casting no shadow. A
'cache' used to be a place where food was stored out of the
reach of wild animals; today it usually refers to a business and
is often preceded by the appropriate product name – hence,
the book cache, the stamp and coin cache. Though many of
the cruder elements of early Alaska have vanished from the
streets of downtown Anchorage, a part of its history lives on
in daily conversation.

Author's note

Following discussion with a fellow student several difficulties remain, as follows:

- From what basis does this student's thinking derive? The main analytical framework needs further clarification to bring out a stronger (sociological) perspective. Moreover, the theme for each paragraph is unclear. What is the purpose of each paragraph?
- In order to achieve this clarification there needs to be a deeper, more explicit, level of analysis to establish how particular examples from the Alaskan experience relate to our understanding of basic social processes. The first two sentences of the first draft hinted at the relationship between language and community membership but this idea has remained undeveloped, even after revision.
- Overall, the second revision provides a lot of evidence but it fails to make a general point. The paragraphs are primarily descriptive lists of colourful Alaskan words and phrases; they now need to be organised thematically, in a more meaningful way.

Draft III

> One of the fundamental institutions which facilitates group identification is language. In acquiring the language of the group, new arrivals not only come to view themselves as group members, but they also become participants in the 'symbolic environment' of the group (Shibutani, 1961:490). Adoption of a common dialect, then, implies identification with the group's history and a shared perception of the group's location in social and cultural space. As Mills (1939:677) writes:

> Along with language we acquire a set of social norms and values. A vocabulary is not merely a string of words; within it are societal textures – institutional and political co-ordinates. Behind every vocabulary lie sets of collective action.

Residents of Anchorage, like those living in regions of the country, employ a vernacular unique to their surroundings, and learning to 'talk like an Alaskan' is the first step in becoming an Alaskan. The evaluative statements implicit in the regional vocabulary of Anchorage residents express three themes: a distinction between those living in Alaska and those living in other areas of the country; a distinction among groups of state residents; and an identification with the state as a whole, rather than with Anchorage itself – a distinction which emphasises the more primitive side of Alaskan life.

One of the first things newcomers to Alaska notice is that virtually all Alaskans refer to non-residents as 'outsiders' and to any place which is not Alaska as 'outside.' These labels, which boast connotations of state chauvinism, form a part of everyday conversation and act as continual reminders that others know very little about Alaska and its ways. Comments like 'outsiders have no way of knowing what we're like' are not infrequently voiced, as local residents are quick to stress the importance of having lived in the state as a necessary precondition of forming opinions about Alaskans. In a similar manner language becomes a vehicle for marking differences between those who merely reside in the state and those who are 'real Alaskans.' The former are called 'cheechakos' and the latter 'sourdoughs,' both linguistic vestiges from the days of the Alaska gold rush.'Cheechako' is a derivative of 'Chicago' and refers to the inexperience displayed by newcomers to Alaska. A sourdough, on the other hand, was a veteran prospector, the name coming from the bread carried on the trail. Because these two terms connote achieved status differences, the words of old-timers are sometimes used to legitimate the claims of individuals or organisations.

Significantly local residents do not refer to themselves as 'Achoragites' for reasons obvious to those who have seen the urban sprawl of Alaska's largest city. A city of 200,000,

Anchorage has been alternatively portrayed as the 'American nightmare' by Norman Mailer and as an 'instant Albuquerque' by John McPhee. Yet despite the presence of glass office buildings, paved streets and residential suburbs, the livelier aspects of Alaska's past live on in the daily conversations. Many of these characterisations have their origin in times when climate played a major role in affecting the course of Alaskan life. The restless, claustrophobic feeling which accompanies the long hours of winter darkness is familiarly known as 'cabin fever' . . . (Cuba, 1984).

Author's Note

- This third draft, while preserving much of the description found in the original paragraph, is more analytical than the original.
- The general significance of the findings has been explained in a new opening paragraph. Sociological references have been added, placing the writing in a contextual framework which is more familiar to a professional audience. The language used is more formal, reflecting a stronger sense of the anticipated audience/readership.
- The second paragraph begins with a revised version of the first sentence of the previous draft, but is followed by a rather long sentence outlining the organisation of the later paragraphs. This provides a thematic guide sorely lacking in the first two versions.
- The examples that appear in the first draft as a long list of descriptive items are now grouped according to what they reveal about Alaskan life. A few more illustrations have been included, but, for the most part, the remaining paragraphs consist of material reorganised from the earlier draft. **Developing this framework carries the previous drafts beyond description to analysis.**

The above example demonstrates the necessity and advantage of approaching the task of writing in a recursive way. Writing at any level involves the processes of drafting, reflection and re-writing, but take heart – as undergraduate students you will not be required, nor will you have the time, for extensive periods of leisurely reflection and revision. Remember that your writing task is finite and has to stop. If nothing else, your hand-in date signals the point at which it must end, at least for this assignment. As a writer you must aim and plan for **closure** but accept that your first draft is never final.

GETTING STARTED

While there is no simple formula for arriving at a writing strategy that is appropriate for everyone, there are things that others have found useful and that you may wish to consider as you develop your own personal approach to writing. These are described below.

Describe and Assess How You Currently Write

Before you can improve your writing, you must know **how** you write. Like a social scientist interested in the rituals of writing (Becker, 1986), begin by identifying how you tackle writing. Consider the following aspects as they apply to you as a student writer:

- When do you first begin to write an essay or report which your tutor has set?
- What day or time of day is usually available for you to write?
- What kinds of equipment, e.g. word processor, typewriter, pen, pencil, do you use?
- Where do you normally write? Is this your first choice? If not, what is?
- Under what circumstances and conditions do you write? Describe problems with other people and/or noise. What is your preferred environment?
- How long is a typical writing session? Is this within your control or controlled by others? Describe the factors which influence the time you can give.
- What form of planning do you adopt for essays and reports?
- What sort of notes do you make? How do you record these and how do you utilise these when writing your assignment?
- How many drafts of an essay would you normally produce before handing it in?

- Do you seek help from others during particular stages of writing? Who are they? Do you exchange drafts or extracts with them?

ACTIVITY: YOUR APPROACH TO WRITING

- Using the above questions, complete a description of how you typically approach your writing task. Consider all aspects, plus details of when, where and how. Produce a short written statement (not more than one side of A4) which accurately captures the context of your writing rituals.
- On the basis of this description, reflect upon your organisation and procedures and evaluate the outcomes. For example, is there a constant pattern to your writing or is there some variation according to the course or module you are taking or the topic type required? What problems have you encountered; what appears to work well and what aspects of your approach would you like to change? Write a short evaluation which identifies your strengths and weaknesses.
- Focus upon those aspects of your approach which you wish to change. Formulate an ACTION PLAN which identifies:
  – a list of things to change
  – ways in which changes can be made
  – a date by which changes are to be completed.
- Compare your experiences with friends on your course. In a relaxed way discuss problems, talk about your anxieties and plan together how you can improve your writing.

Working your way through these activities will not only give you **strategies for improving** your writing task, but will help you take significant steps towards demystifying the process of writing.

Start Early

It is virtually impossible to begin working on paper too soon. Revisions take a lot of time, and yet they are indispensable if you are going to use the process of writing as a tool for analysis in social science. Once you incorporate revising into your definition of writing, the various writing tasks – reports, book reviews, notes for oral presentations, essays and dissertations – should improve, and you will find that allowing time for revising is no less important than spending long hours in the library preparing to write.

When you know what writing you are required to do and are clear on the dates for its completion, it is important to begin thinking about how you will approach it. What will be your main focus? What theoretical frameworks will you use? What other sources of information will you need to consult in order to make progress with this assignment? Talk about your ideas with your tutor and with other students in your lecture or seminar groups, or with other friends. Most importantly, make notes on your ideas for the writing task and try to establish a rough outline or plan which will provide you with a basis upon which to organise, select and prioritise your contents. This early writing, collecting information and deciding upon an appropriate approach, will help you to become more familiar with the process of objectifying (and thereby clarifying) your thoughts.

Keep thinking about the task in hand. **Write down your ideas** and keep your notes, observations and other research materials readily to hand. This way, when you start to write a draft of your assignment you will not be starting cold. Rather, you will find, to your pleasant surprise, that you have been writing all along!

Read With a Critical Eye

Every day we read many different kinds of writing – newspapers, magazines, novels, textbooks. Some we read for pleasure, some because they are required. We skim some and plod through others, but, in general, we think of reading in terms of what substantive information it offers us: a review of a film we may want to see, an interesting point to pursue in a journal article, or a detailed analysis of some public issue. If we find what we read useful or interesting, it is usually because it contains what we were looking for. In short, it fulfils our expectations about **content**.

In contrast, our interest in what we are reading may stem from **how** it is written. A clever organising scheme, an unusual choice of words, or an illuminating analogy can appeal to us regardless of content. In these instances we are admiring someone's expertise **as a writer**.

As you read, make a point of paying close attention to what you like and what you dislike about a particular piece of writing. Successful, professional writing in social science normally displays high standards of content and process elements and you may learn a lot from such writing, particularly by developing an awareness of how others deal with issues of audience, style, presentation of argument and the achievement of synthesis. Think how you might incorporate these techniques into your own approach to writing.

Learn Word-Processing Skills

Word processing has transformed the way many of us write. Words, sentences and paragraphs can be easily moved within a single document, or from one document to another. Clean drafts can be generated whenever they are needed. Complex formatting procedures, such as justification, centring or footnoting, require only a few keystrokes. Because word-processing software often comes with a variety of specialised sub-programmes, you can also use it to check your manuscript for spelling errors, to substitute one word for another using a thesaurus programme or to compile a list of references using an appropriate style. All of these facilities increase the ease with which you can revise and improve your work. They also enable you to exchange writing assignments for review and revision with your peers or tutor, without adding the time-consuming burden of re-typing each draft.

Even if you are a complete beginner, learning a word-processing programme is not too difficult. In most universities and institutions of higher education, access to such programmes is readily available and positively encouraged. You are strongly advised to find out, from computer advisory or library staff, about any training programmes offered, and to take active steps to develop your word-processing skills.

If you have your own personal computer (P.C.), you can of course select any word-processing software which is compatible with your machine, but where possible you should aim for compatibility with your university or college system. This will enable you to transfer your work from home to your place of study without difficulty and at the same time will provide access to the institution's printing facilities. If you are considering buying your own P.C. and you can afford to do so, it is best to choose a recent model which has common software rather than a 'dedicated' machine, e.g. an Amstrad, use of which is restricted as it is incompatible with other systems. Irrespective of the ownership of equipment, the important thing is to be a 'user'.

Develop Your Editorial Skills

To reap the benefits of reflecting, re-thinking and re-writing, you must become a good editor. In the first stages this means that you should become used to re-reading your drafts and seeing whether your writing communicates the main ideas clearly and directly. It is very helpful if you work with others on this. Read and comment on an essay or part of an essay written by one of your friends. What advice can you give? Is it clear? Does it make sense? What is the main focus? How can it be improved? Later, you will be concerned with more detail, checking for clarity, conciseness and grammatical style, sentence by sentence. You will want to ensure that the organisation, balance and content of the essay is sound. In this way you will begin to acquire effective editorial skills. (Further suggestions concerning both specific and general revisions are considered in Chapter Seven.)

This process characterises professional practice. Social scientists, like those in other academic circles, read and comment on each other's writing. You may have noticed that authors of books and articles which you have encountered in your research usually acknowledge the assistance of others. Some of the editorial insights that emerge in a piece of writing are the author's; some come from readers; and some, often the most helpful, result from discussion with colleagues. Enlisting the aid of a circle of editorial friends can improve your writing immeasurably, but make sure that there is a genuine exchange of work and remember to give appropriate credit for any editorial suggestions that you eventually adopt.

If you receive an edited copy of your work from someone else, ask your 'editor' for specific information about your paper's major weaknesses. Don't feel that you have to agree with all the comments you receive. Your reservations may, in fact, generate a productive debate about your writing which leads to rethinking and revision in another direction. **The primary purpose of editing is to open up a dialogue, not simply to acquiesce to the suggestions of others.**

If you are editing your own work – and all writers must develop the habit of editing their own work – you need to develop ways of distancing yourself from your writing. One simple step in that direction involves transferring your writing from one medium to another. Readers, as well as authors, respond quite differently to typewritten copies of the same material. If you usually draft papers in longhand, try typing them before editing. 'Transcribing' your writing in this manner provides an alternative context for your words that is essential in objectifying your thoughts. Of course, allowing ample time for writing and editing is crucial to this process. That is why it is impossible to overstate the need to start writing early.

Learn From Your Peers

Sometimes, you may be reluctant to discuss set assignments with your peers; perhaps you fear that your close collaboration on writing tasks may make it difficult to distinguish your work from that of others and hence make you vulnerable to charges of plagiarism. This problem is discussed more fully in Chapter Six, but it is important to emphasise here that tutors in most universities and colleges encourage their students to discuss and comment on each other's writing. From your point of view it is important to acknowledge any suggestions which you include in the essay, report or dissertation. A small friendship circle from your lecture or seminar groups can provide enormous levels of support and critical appraisals of your writing, but remember, always acknowledge your sources!

'I Don't Know Enough'

Sometimes, identification with, and knowledge of, contemporary fields of study in social science can present problems. This may be due to a lack of confidence in your ability to understand relevant theories and build up a sufficient fund of knowledge and awareness in your subject. Alternatively, you may feel uncertain of your identity and place as a student in your new subject area. Where confidence is in short supply, you feel unfamiliar with the leading theorists and the main writers in your field, whereas 'everyone else' seems to 'know' so much more. Such feelings are most common with first-year students but they can affect second- and third-year students as well, particularly if you are going through a difficult phase in your course of study. Confidence, by its nature, is an individual matter and there are no easy solutions to lack of confidence. However, the specialised knowledge, concepts and methods of social science need not be sources of alienating jargon and confusion if you can regard these elements as resources for your use. In time, and with practice, you will become more familiar with the language of discourse and make it your own. A way of addressing these problems is indicated below.

ACTIVITY: PEER SUPPORT FOR WRITING

Your writing development skills can benefit from discussion with student friends on your course or module. You might wish to start by talking to two or three of your immediate friends about your current essay assignment or project report.

Some specific points you might want to consider include:

- Your plan or outline for the essay
- The theoretical perspectives you intend to use
- Reading already completed; further reading you will need to do
- Additional, more specific information you might need.

The important thing is to start discussing and to take advantage of the support and clarification such a group offers. You may find that the group works well together, and decide to meet more regularly to discuss other writing tasks.

2. The Management of Writing

Effective writing is part of a wider set of intellectual and organising skills which you will need to acquire in order to address successfully your role and responsibilities as a student of social science. It is difficult to imagine someone who writes convincingly throughout their undergraduate course of study yet who at the same time conveys an image of personal disorganisation and ineffectual study. **Effective writing is integral to being an effective student.** In order to achieve it you need to acquire actively strategies for the management of your studies generally and your writing assignments in particular.

This chapter aims to put your writing tasks into context, before examining in greater detail how efficient, confident management of library resources can enhance the quality and level of writing and contribute to your sense of identity as a student of social science. It is particularly appropriate if you are beginning your studies in social science.

BECOMING ORGANISED

Personal organisation is a familiar theme when you first arrive at university or college and begin the difficult task of making sense of your new surroundings and accepting the challenge of learning in higher education. The following, simple exercise will enable you to quickly confirm whether or not your life as a student is sufficiently organised for effective study.

ACTIVITY: HOW ORGANISED ARE YOU?

Use the following checklist to help you decide whether your life is organised for efficiency. Place a tick beside those questions to which your answer is **yes**.

Can you find last week's lecture notes and class notes
in two minutes?

How many times in the last week have you intended
to do something but not done it?

Do you usually get to appointments, classes, lectures and
tutorials on time?

How many times have you skipped meals because you have
not bought any food?

Is getting ready to leave always a rush?

Do you search for wearable clothes, wash quickly and
hastily, grab a cup of tea and dash out of the door?

Source: University of Sunderland, 1993

Your answers will indicate whether your level of organisation and planning is working for you. If you never have enough food, are late for appointments, can't find your notes and generally miss out on doing things you want to do and have planned to do, it is unlikely that you will be in a position to organise your writing assignments so that they will be completed on time. In these circumstances you need to re-assesses your organisation and introduce some structure into your life. If, on the other hand, you find that you are generally well organised, use this as a basis for developing, improving and becoming more successful in your study and writing skills.

STARTING TO PLAN

Whatever stage in your studies you have reached and whatever your previous experience, planning is a crucial element. This process usually starts

ACTIVITY: TIME-TABLING

Using the blank timetable below, identify your weekly activities. First, fill in:

- Your formal learning commitments during the week, that is, lectures, seminars, tutorials and workshops you must attend
- Times for lunch and evening meals (remember you may wish to use some of these as peer tutorials, to discuss your writing with other students)
- Any regular leisure activity you intend to pursue
- Other commitments, family, full/part-time job

TIME TABLE

	8	9	10	11	12	1	2	3	4	5	6	7	8	9
Monday														
Tuesday														
Wednesday														
Thursday														
Friday														
Saturday														
Sunday														

Source: University of Sunderland, 1993

by deciding what you need to do, what your commitments are and when you will be required to complete your tasks. First, look at the time that is already committed and that you cannot re-allocate. Depending upon your personal circumstances, i.e. whether you are studying on a full- or part-time basis, this can include time spent as follows: (University of Sunderland, 1993):

- Formal teaching/learning situations
- Family commitments
- Travelling, meals and leisure activities
- Full/part-time job

Now it is possible to plan more individual studies or learning time. This will vary between individuals and according to the area of study, but as a guide, a full-time social science student with 12 hours per week of formal teaching/learning time will normally be expected to allocate 18 hours of additional personal study time, giving a total of 30 hours of academic work. This figure is a minimum recommendation which may need to be increased at particular times, for example when you are preparing for examinations or when you are involved in time-consuming field research. Even so, following this form of planning routine and making your commitments explicit, it is quite possible to fit everything in and still enjoy an evening out and have a pleasant night's sleep! When such schedules are not organised or when they are ignored, you risk having 'no time' to write your essays, complaining of your tutor's unreasonable demands and becoming 'stressed out'!

MANAGING YOUR TIME

Organising your study time involves identifying everything you have to do, selecting what is of particular importance and deciding how and when to carry out particular tasks. A common method is to prioritise each task according to its importance and urgency.

ACTIVITY: PRIORITISING YOUR TASKS

- List all the tasks you know that you have to complete over the next two or three weeks. Include both study assignments and social and family commitments.
- Now prioritise these tasks by placing a number (1) next to the most important and (2) by the next most important and so on. If you find that you have put a (1) by several items, adding **A**, **B** or **C** may help in finally establishing the order of priorities.

The following is a list of tasks that one student had to do over the period of a week:

1   Reading assignment for sociology seminar, Tues p.m.
2   Students union equal opportunities committee meeting
3   Meet friend at station, Thursday a.m.
4   Complete social policy essay, Wednesday
5   Write up Monday's lecture notes
6   Go to the library, project research
7   Prepare book review
8   Meet landlord to negotiate rental agreement
9   Go to bank to discuss overdraft account
10 Prepare examination revision schedule for next month

Develop a list which fits your needs and priorities:

LEARNING TO LEARN

More than ever as a student in higher education you are being encouraged to take responsibility for your own learning; the idea is that while there may be less teaching, more learning will occur. While a major factor in this is financial resources, it makes good educational sense to develop successfully greater control over your own learning, and you become competent in learning from your experience.

In order to survive and indeed prosper in these new circumstances, you will first need to develop a strong and effective study and writing skills base; it is important to your success in any subject area that you learn how to learn. There is a growing and sometimes confusing amount of literature in the 'how to study/write' field. Some of these works may be of interest, particularly if you require more detailed information and advice than it is possible to give within the context of this book. The recommendations for further reading in Appendix I is a selective rather than a definitive list and is divided into those works with a clear subject orientation and those providing more practical self-help which have been developed by some universities to support the learning needs of their expanding and diverse student populations.

It is important to emphasise that in developing your study skills, you should first discover what materials and resources are available in your own university or college; ask your subject tutors and personal tutors for advice and consult with members of the library staff.

Beginning Writing

Most of us find it difficult to get down to studying, especially if we are engaged in writing an assignment within strict time limits. Much displacement activity can take place. For example, it becomes crucially important to re-arrange the contents of your files; you suddenly remember an urgent 'phone call you simply have to make, you decide that you can't start without a cup of tea – anything that delays the moment of beginning to write. **The only way to start is to start**, but here are some strategies which might start you off:

- Tell yourself that you are just doing a draft which (by definition) need not be perfect; write 'draft' at the top of your first page.
- Start somewhere other than at the beginning and come back to the opening paragraph.
- Try to explain out loud to yourself, or someone else if possible, how you are going to approach your writing task.

- Use a word processor so that you can easily change or delete what you have written.
- Begin with something you feel knowledgeable and confident about.
- Give yourself a set time for your writing, avoiding sessions which are unrealistically lengthy; aim for a productive period of one hour before taking a break.

Reflecting on Your Writing

An important part of the approach to writing described in this book is the process of reflection. As a reflective writer it is important to be *critical* (as opposed to *negative*) about the knowledge, theories and values which you encounter during your course or programme of study. This involves a 'dialogue' between you and the lecturer and the course contents which you are 'offered'. It emphasises your responsibility to be an active learner, to establish the validity of these contents in a meaningful way. You can do this by reflecting on your learning experiences, for instance by:

- Thinking about the relationship between particular forms of knowledge and theory and their wider context; i.e., where do things fit? What links exist between different areas of study? What is the broader picture?
- Evaluating the validity of what you have been told or read, i.e., does it seem appropriate? What evidence is there to support a particular view?
- Trying to envisage other possibilities – what different explanations are feasible?

These are some of the elements of reflection which form part of what your tutors mean when they encourage you to be critical or analytical. Being self-critical in this way will lead you to regard the experience of your lectures, seminars and tutorials in a more objective way – that is:

> 'As a social scientist you have to control this rather elaborate inter-play, to capture what you experience and sort it out; only in this way can you hope to use it to guide and test your reflection and in the process shape yourself as an intellectual craftsman (*sic*).'
>
> (Mills, 1970, p. 216)

A Reflective Journal

How is it possible to utilise your learning experiences? One method is to keep a journal and there are various forms this can take. For example, your journal can be used to monitor your progress on the various courses you are taking. This will involve writing about the assignments and activities which you are doing and recording and evaluating your responses. In other words, your journal is not simply a diary in which you record the events of the day, rather it is a way of seeking to evaluate your responses and assess how effective you have been in particular situations, perhaps as a contributor to a seminar discussion, as a note-taker in a main lecture or as library researcher, collecting material for your next essay.

Reflecting on your work in this way will enable you to monitor your current performance and progress and provide you with a basis on which to plan ahead and make necessary adjustments and changes to improve your responses.

Given the very considerable pressures which derive from undergraduate (modular) programmes, keeping a regular and detailed journal should not be seen as an extra item of work; it is a crucial means of becoming a more effective learner, as you self-consciously address the issues of time-management, goal-setting and the assessment of the strengths and weaknesses of your performance. In this way you can begin to exert control and manage your own learning. In summary, writing a journal will enable you to:

- Record a personal statement comprising a range of issues, ideas, thoughts and plans which emerge from your course of study or from the wider context of your life in higher education. These are your own observations and do not form part of assessed work, but there may be occasions when your journal entries can be used as a basis for discussion with fellow students and tutors.
- Identify questions you may wish to raise about particular areas of your work – for example, things you encounter in your reading, essay writing and seminar discussions.
- Develop the activity of your writing on a regular basis, in a comfortable and stress-free context.
- Monitor your progress and evaluate how effectively you are responding to the demands and requirements of a particular course.

Your journal can be enormously helpful in allowing you to distance yourself from your academic work and objectify your experiences; to reflect on the progress you are making and to evaluate the action you need to take in order to improve. It is an important part of gaining more control over your own learning.

USING THE LIBRARY

Irrespective of the form your writing takes, you will need to spend time researching in the library. It is important to emphasise that time spent in this way is not only something you do before you begin to write, but is integral to the process of writing itself.

Libraries and library research have changed dramatically in recent years, largely through technological and computer-based advances which have been integrated into libraries in a variety of ways. It is important to appreciate that many libraries have the capacity to provide access to catalogues in other libraries in different parts of the country. More than ever libraries are not just repositories of books, journals and newspapers; they are gateways, providing access to information and networks beyond their own sites and individual collections.

All this means that your capacity to search for information has greatly expanded. It is therefore important that you acquire an understanding of how computer technology can be used for bibliographic research, if you are to control the vast amounts of information these technologies generate. The remainder of this chapter provides a selective overview of the library materials most often used by social scientists and how you can best manage some of these processes; but first let's consider some points of general guidance.

DEVELOPING LIBRARY SKILLS

It is important to approach library research with a realistic set of assumptions and expectations. Even a modest library collection has an enormous amount of potentially relevant material and it will require time, patience and understanding on your part, to identify and obtain the materials you require. As you work towards becoming more efficient and effective in library research methods, the following guidelines should be helpful:

- **Create and plan a schedule and keep to it!** Library research is a creative task for which you must take responsibility. Unlike going to a lecture which has been planned by your tutor, the onus is much more on you to devise how best to spend your hours; for this to be effective, you should develop a research plan and take full benefit of the time you spend in the library.
- **Allow plenty of time.** It is most likely that things will take longer than you had anticipated. For example, you may identify a key reference to a journal article that your library does not have in stock but is able to obtain through an interlending system. Inevitably, this will take time, so it is advisable to plan generously.
- **Develop a balanced approach.** Half a day is probably insufficient time for bibliographic research, while half a term is probably excessive. You should guard against turning library research into an exercise that becomes an end in itself rather than a means to an end. It can provide you with a compelling rationalisation for not writing, i.e. 'I don't know enough to begin'. Develop a balance between gathering, analysing and writing about library source materials. You cannot expect to make the best use of what you collect if you are still seeking new material a few days before your essay is due.
- **Keep a record of your library research.** It is difficult to know exactly what materials you will incorporate into your final essay, so at this stage you must document everything . Keep (brief) accurate notes of the materials you come across and most importantly, always record the full reference of the book, journal article or paper. This will save you an enormous amount of time (as well as anxiety) later on.
- **Develop a research vocabulary.** Like published social sciences research, library reference works rely on vocabularies that convey large amounts of information in relatively little space. Finding your way through the large stocks of information which libraries hold requires learning several methods because research guides do not employ a standard vocabulary or format.

Some sources are prepared by the library itself and are confined solely to the materials held by that library; others are commercial databases brought in to provide indexing services on a much larger scale than the library could produce for itself. Although books, journal articles and papers traced in this way are not necessarily items that the library holds in stock, they can probably be obtained for you through an interlending scheme, e.g. that of the British Library.

Before searching you should begin developing a list of research terms or keywords which define and encompass your subject. Because arrangements and vocabulary vary so much between databases, whether printed or in computerised format, you need to include synonyms (alternative words for the elements in your topic-related terms), American words and spellings and broader and narrower terms. To help you in this a database may have a thesaurus that provides a list of subject headings assigned to each item, showing the preferred indexing term and often giving you alternative related, broader and narrower terms in use in your field of research.

- **Ask for help when you need it.** Don't hesitate to ask a librarian for assistance. They are familiar with reference works, abstracts and indexes, computer databases, and other resources in their collection. They will be able to match your topic to the appropriate sources so that you can make the best use of your research time.
- **Recognise and utilise the diversity of libraries.** Although there are broad similarities, not all libraries are alike. For example, public libraries, especially large central ones, offer a wide range of books and reference works. Equally important is the access they offer to reserve stocks of material both locally and nationally, through their own interlending service. For many assignments, projects, local and regional cultural studies, the public library can be a valuable starting point in your research.
- **Utilise specialist resources.** Specialist libraries offer a rich source of material. When you have reached the point in your researches when you need to look beyond the scope of your university or college library, and following discussion and advice from your tutor, you may find it useful to consult a specialist library, though normally this will be in connection with a project or final dissertation rather than routine essays and reports.

LIBRARIES AND COMPUTERS

Libraries and computers have a symbiotic relationship. As repositories of vast quantities of detailed, structured information, libraries are constantly changing and expanding. Computers, because of their ability to store large quantities of information and to edit, update, and retrieve this information quickly and easily, are well suited to manipulating bibliographic entries. In short, computers have changed the way libraries are organised, allowing for new and unprecedented ways of handling both printed and electronic information.

Virtually every aspect of information management in libraries has been touched by computer technology. Many important indexes and abstracts, statistical data and even the full text of journals and newspapers are now available as databases, either interactively on-line or in CD-ROM (compact disc-read only memory format). Computer technology allows you to cover vast quantities of citations in seconds, to tailor your search in a variety of ways not possible in print formats, and to obtain the most recent information. Library catalogues can be accessed through computer terminals, sometimes distributed throughout the campus, providing more information (e.g. whether or not the book is on loan or available on the shelves) and more extensive methods of searching than older forms of catalogue. It is often possible to print out information from a computer database, or to download it on to your floppy disk.

This widespread incorporation of computer technology into libraries has introduced both benefits and liabilities into library research. On the one hand, computers have expanded the scope of materials that can be searched and the precision with which they can be retrieved, accomplishing both tasks with remarkable speed. On the other hand, the sheer volume of material available through computer searching can easily overwhelm even experienced researchers; moreover, generating useful bibliographic references requires basic skills, instruction and documentation on how the new systems work.

Establishing Your Search Terms

One of the most significant technological advances in indexing is the ability to provide 'keyword' access to information. Keywords are significant words that the computer searches for within specified fields of text, such as in the titles or abstracts of journal citations. Even using keywords, it is still possible to generate vast quantities of information. It is therefore necessary to conduct a *strategic search* that will produce more relevant and specific information. To do this you will first need to identify appropriate keywords. Consider the following example involving research for an essay:

> **subject of essay:** business structures within ethnic minority communities in the U.K.
> **possible keywords:** ethnic minorities; business.

The next step is to establish some relationship between these keywords. This can be done quite simply by deciding what form of data you wish to have. For example, is it sufficient to have references on just **one** of your keywords? If so your instructions can be given as follows:

minority OR business.

It is important to realise that referring to terms in this way means that only one of the keywords has to be present for the reference to be retrieved. Hence **this strategy broadens the range of references that will result.**

Alternatively, you may be working in an information-rich area and thus find it is important to focus your search as closely as possible, proceeding as follows:

minority AND business.

When you combine terms like this both have to be present for the reference to be retrieved, i.e. this form of instruction will only retrieve those items containing both words and in this way serves to limit the range of references. This method of searching relies on the use of **Logical Operators**, i.e. **OR; AND; NOT.** (The latter term can be used to limit the range.) Generally, however, it is most effective to use the operator 'AND' together with two or more keywords.

One of the main advantages of using computer databases is the way in which search terms can be combined to produce very specific results. Searches can be refined further by specifying limits within particular areas of study, for example, for dates, language or geographical location.

Exactly what you will be able to do in a search depends on the scope and structure of the particular database in which you are working and the library resources available to you. There are many exciting technological developments now taking place with increasing numbers of on-line information services which can be accessed via terminals in (university) libraries. Frequently, these services are being offered on an institutional subscription basis so there are no costs incurred by you as the 'end user'. In these circumstances it is possible to conduct the search yourself without worrying unduly about the time spent on-line.

It is most important that you make early contact with your college or university library to find out what services are offered so that you can take maximum advantage. Library staff are vital allies in your undergraduate studies and you should endeavour to establish effective relationships.

Journals

There are huge numbers of journals published world-wide. Ulrich's international periodicals directory 1993-94, Bowker-Saur, lists over 140,000 titles of periodicals in all fields, which appear at both regular and irregular intervals, and provides subject access to them. It also indicates whether they are covered by any abstracting and indexing services.

Any individual library service can only purchase a small number of these titles, and it is usually impracticable for libraries to index the contents of their own periodicals stock to any significant degree. You are unlikely, for instance, to find details of individual articles on the library catalogue. For this reason, libraries place equal emphasis on the provision of tools, known as abstracts and indexes, which enable you to search for articles and book reviews, under subject, or by author or title, from a far larger range of journals than your library can take.

Libraries purchase a range of indexes to supply this need, choosing between a variety of formats: printed, CD ROM or on-line. Each one deals with a broad subject area, such as Social Sciences, Womens Studies,

Anthropology or Economics, and will provide indexing to at least some of the more important journals within that subject. Abstracts are sometimes included; these are summaries of the content of each article or review, sometimes quite substantial in length, giving you a good idea of how useful the item might be to you.

Once you have traced suitable references, you will need to refer back to your own library's catalogue to check whether the relevant journals are taken there. If not, you may be able to get them via inter-library loans services.

When using any index, make sure you know what period it covers. Unless you are only interested in the most current writing in your field, you will usually want to trace several years back. Print versions often appear at regular intervals throughout the year, quarterly or bi-monthly for example, and then cumulate into an annual volume. Each issue will only cover material published within that period. CD ROMs, although they have the capacity to store very large quantities of information, do not necessarily have more than one year's worth of references on each disk, although they often do. You may need to consult several to cover the ground. Even on-line you may need to swop between years as you search.

It is always advisable to ascertain the scope and purpose of the index before you use it. This can be done by consulting the preface or introduction in the front of printed indexes, which will also tell you how to use the index, and give a list of the journals covered.

The field is changing fast with the advent of widespread access to databases via computer. Libraries currently offer a judicious mix of databases and formats, but as the means of delivery of information develop and costs come down, this situation may alter.

Getting Started: Vocabulary and Concepts

Although you cannot expect to know precisely what library materials will be most relevant for your project until you begin your research, the nature of your assignment and the subject or topic area will enable you to direct your efforts. A good place to start is with specialised encyclopedias and dictionaries which address particular topics within a discipline and provide more than brief definitions of social science concepts. Specialised dictionaries and encyclopedias offer background discussions of the major issues and problems within a particular subject area. They use the formal language of academic writers who are expert in their areas and provide you with an early opportunity to become familiar with the 'language of discourse' in your subject area and a basis upon which you can develop your own specialist terminology.

In addition to providing sources of direct information, these works of reference are often followed by selective bibliographies that include many references not directly discussed by the author. These can be used to initiate your library research since they are likely to include significant research conducted on the topic before the entry was written. However, because these volumes are not revised frequently, you should turn to other sources for brief overviews of more contemporary research. Recently published textbooks often include up-to-date bibliographies as do periodic reviews of the literature (for example, the *Annual Review of Anthropology*). Similiar reviews are available in psychology and sociology.

Each discipline has at least one major dictionary and encyclopedia that can help you start your library research. For example:

Anthropology: *The Macmillan Dictionary of Anthropology* (1986). London: Macmillan.

Economics: *The New Palgrave. A Dictionary of Economics* (1987). London: Macmillan.

Bannock, G., Baxter, R., & Davis, E. *The Penguin Dictionary of Economics (Fifth Edition)* (1992).

Psychology: Bruno, F. (1986). *A Dictionary of Key Words in Psychology*. London: Routledge.

Reber, A.S. (1986). *Penguin Dictionary of Psychology*. Harmondsworth: Penguin

Politics: Miller, D. et.al. (1986). *An Encyclopedia Dictionary of Political Thought*. Oxford: Blackwell

Sociology: Abercrombie, N. Hill, S., Turner, B.S. (1988) *The Penguin Dictionary of Sociology (Second Edition)*. Harmondsworth: Penguin.

Boudon, R. and Bourricaud, F. (1989) *A Critical Dictionary of Sociology*. London: Tavistock.

A useful source of reference found in most libraries is *The International Encyclopedia of the Social Sciences* (1968), New York: Free Press.

INDEXES AND ABSTRACTS

Indexes and abstracts are probably the most important bibliographical tools of the social scientist. Like dictionaries and encyclopedias these reference works are specialised guides to the vast range of topics of interest to social scientists, covered in journals. But unlike dictionaries, indexes and abstracts go beyond brief introductions by helping you identify research that has been conducted upon a topic in which you are interested. Importantly, they are compiled frequently so that they contain the most recently published research. Computers have assisted this process, greatly reducing the time between the publication of an article and its appearance in an abstract or index; and enabling regular updating. Although many of the indexes and abstracts are available through searches of on-line databases and CD Rom, it is important to know how to conduct a bibliographic search using the printed versions of these materials, if only because you may find yourself working in a library where computerised searches are either too difficult or too costly to arrange.

DATABASES

Studying and researching in social science you will encounter a number of general databases but below we consider two systems which you will find particularly relevant and useful.

Applied Social Science Index and Abstracts

The *Applied Social Science Index and Abstract* (ASSIA) is published quarterly and covers some 550+ journals from Britain and America. It is a British publication and provides highly relevant references for the British experience in the fields of social services, economics, penal services, politics, employment, race relations, health and education. ASSIA can be searched on Data-Star (file name ASSIA) and is also available on CD ROM as 'ASSIA plus'.

Social Sciences Citations Index (SSCI)

The Social Sciences Citations Index (SSCI) is a very large database comprising some 1,400 titles. Because it is computer generated (available via Dialog, BRS and DIMDI as well as on CD ROM and via BRS on-line) the SSCI indexes more journals than most other reference works and it does so fairly quickly, making it a good print source for identifying relatively recent research. It is, however, constructed on somewhat different lines from other indexes and is divided into three different parts:

- **Permuterm index**, which lists entries by subject keywords.
- **Source index**, listing articles arranged by author.
- **Citation index**, library authors cited in footnotes of published work.

When using the SSCI you should first consult your librarian to gain an understanding of the main principles upon which the index is based. One of the key concepts is citation searching and this generic system is now briefly discussed.

CITATION SEARCHING

Citation searching provides a mechanism for identifying articles that have cited or referenced a known work (journal article, book, etc.). This may be useful because articles which cite the same reference are likely to be about a similar or related area of research. Cross-referencing in this way makes it possible to find articles of interest that may not be found by any other method.

An important work is likely to be referenced by a large number of articles. Citation searching can be used to identify works that have been cited a large number of times and which might therefore be of particular interest or relevance.

Each cited reference has a standard layout:

- **Author** of the cited reference.
- **Year** the reference was published.

- **Volume** and **page** number of the reference.
- **Journal** or other **work** in which reference was published.

When articles are displayed the cited references are always shown in a standard form. For example, a reference to an article written by G Wilson in the 1993 edition of the *Journal of European Social Policy* (Vol. 3 (2) p. 91) will be displayed as:

Wilson, G. 1993 Vol. 3 (2) p. 91 J. of European Social Policy.

Some references do not include all this information. In particular, for certain kinds of reference (for example, standard publications) there may not be an author name. These are labelled '**anonymous citations**' as opposed to '**authored citations**'.

When searching for authored citations some or all of the fields may by used, depending on the amount of information that can be supplied. Note that in many systems only the name of the first author appears in citation, other author names are not supplied.

GOVERNMENT PUBLICATIONS

These are an essential source of information for social scientists. They are often referred to as HMSO (Her Majesty's Stationery Office) publications, although this is not strictly accurate as not all official publications are in fact published by the Stationery Office.

This type of literature covers a very wide range of material. It is divided into Parliamentary and non-Parliamentary publications, the working documents departments. From the two categories of publication you will probably use, in particular, reports from committees and commissions, annual reports, policy papers, statistical series, parliamentary debates and Acts of Parliament.

Parliamentary Papers

These fall into several series, some of which are described below. Each series has its own distinct numbering system and as Parliamentary Papers are usually housed in a separate sequence in libraries, this is often the shelf reference number that you will need to take from the library catalogue.

Bills, Acts and Records of Debates

A Bill is a draft version of proposed legislation which, if it passes successfully through its various stages and is approved by both Houses, becomes an Act of Parliament. These are called Public General Acts and are cited using a short title, year and chapter number, as follows:

> Children Act 1989 (C41)

Debates in the House of Commons and the Lords are recorded in two separate series of Hansard (House of Commons/Lords Parliamentary Debates) which appears daily, weekly and then in bound volumes, with appropriate indexes.

House of Commons and House of Lords Papers

These are numbered using HC or HL prefixing the parliamentary session and running number, as follows:

> HC 622 1989-90 National Audit Office Homelessness

Command Papers

Command papers are an interesting group comprising, among other things, policy papers, otherwise known as 'white papers'; reports; some statistical series such as criminal statistics; and some annual reports, such as Prison Statistics.

Many important reports appear as Command Papers, although others are published as non-parliamentary papers. The reports of Royal Commissions however, are always published as Command Papers. These are set up to carry out investigation prior to the formulation of legislation. They are often referenced by the name of the chair, for example:

> Beveridge Report (Report on Social Insurance and Allied
> Services, 1942)

Command papers are identified by numbers comprising a combination of letters from the word 'Command', such as Cd or Comnd, and a running number, for example:

> Cmd 6404 (Beveridge Report) 1942
> Cmnd 5256 (The Channel Tunnel Project) 1973
> Cm 1599 (The Citizen's Charter) 1991

Note, however, that these numbers do not relate to any particular parliamentary session.

Non-Parliamentary Publications

Apart from Statutory Instruments, which are orders with the force of law made under powers delegated to departments by Parliament, these comprise reports and information publications. 'Green Papers' can be either parliamentary or non-parliamentary publications and are statements of proposals put forward by government for general discussion in the country.

STATISTICS

You will find various sources particularly useful:
- **Central Statistical Office's Guide to Official Statistics.** This CSO guide confirms that the statistics have been compiled and where they have been published.
- **Annual Abstract of Statistics**, published by the Government's Statistical Service. This contains a selection of tables covering most areas and is a good place to begin.
- **Central Statistical Blue Book.** National Accounts.
- **Employment Gazette.** This is the official journal of the Dept. of Employment and is published monthly.
- **Social Security Statistics** is published annually by HMSO on behalf of the Dept. of Social Security.

It requires experience and patience on your part, together with the assistance of a librarian, to find your way through the wealth of material in the official publications section of your library. Do persevere – they provide valuable contextual information as well as primary data.

'THE LIBRARY DOESN'T HAVE IT'

For various reasons your library may not have the books, journal articles or government reports that you require. However, as we have discussed, a network of reciprocal borrowing exists and, hence, it is unnecessary for each library to strive to hold everything. The system of higher education in this country benefits from an inter-library loan service through the British Library and it is possible to obtain most references you will need through this method. However, obtaining source material by this system will take time, anything from two to five weeks, so it is very important that you allow a sufficient amount of time for the loan process to be completed, and that you make quite sure that the item is essential for the completion of your writing assignment.

DEVELOPING YOUR MAP OF SPECIALIST KNOWLEDGE

Being a student in social science presents you with the opportunity and the challenge of developing specialist knowledge in a particular field. This exciting prospect can create tensions and difficulties, especially when you are setting out on your studies, convinced of your inadequate knowledge and 'terrorised by the literature' (Becker, 1986). Effective use of library resources, developing a familiarity with the physical fabric of your particular shelf or stack area and establishing relationships with the library staff are important constituents of your study world; this is the context in which you will consciously seek to develop proficiency, skill and expertise. As the months go by and you tackle successive writing assignments, you will become increasingly 'at home' in the library and more confident and competent in executing your library research. Your sense of intellectual identity will develop and grow. For a few important hours each week you will give your full attention to the construction of a personal intellectual field; your other roles, as mother, sister, daughter, partner, are displaced as you 'become' a student of social science.

A FINAL COMMENT: FAMILIAR TERRAIN

In each subject area there are a number of journals which help to give shape and identity to particular fields of enquiry. Some of these journals, which are read by professional social scientists, are listed below; they are included here to give you some basis for evaluating the materials you locate – an article appearing in one of these journals has been granted a certain legitimacy by its particular discipline. Moreover, several journals are the official publications of major professional associations – for example, *Sociology* is the journal of the British Sociological Association. As you research into the issues and problems of your area you will routinely encounter these and other journals. They will become familiar and will help you to strengthen your map of specialist knowledge.

Anthropology
American Anthropologist
Annual Review of Anthropology
Antiquity
Cambridge Archaeological Journal
Current Anthropology
Journal of Anthropological Research

Economics
American Economic Review
Applied Economics
British Review of Economic Issues
Cambridge Journal of Economics
Developing Economic Review
Oxford Review of Economic Policy

Politics
American Journal of Political Science
Policy and Politics
Political Quarterly
Political Studies
Politics and Society
West European Politics

Psychology
British Journal of Psychology
Journal of Applied Psychology
Journal of Personality and Social Psychology
Psychological Bulletin
Psychological Review

Sociology
American Sociological Review
British Journal of Sociology
Critical Social Policy
European Journal of Sociology
Sociological Quarterly
Sociological Review
Sociology

As your research moves from its general beginning to more specific, research-orientated references, the following sources will help you to locate theses, conference reports and current research.

LIBRARIES AND INFORMATION UNITS

- **The Association for Information Management (ASLIB)** directory of information sources in the United Kingdom is regularly updated and covers government departments, trade and professional associations, charitable bodies and educational establishments, as well as a wide variety of interest groups and special collections. It has a comprehensive subject index and gives details of access.

- **The British Library Guide** to libraries and information units in government departments and other organisations is regularly updated and covers in particular government departments and other official and semi-official bodies, including overseas government agencies. It gives comprehensive details of the type of stock and subjects covered and access information. There are descriptions of the collections of all the departments of the British Library, such as the Newspaper Library, the India Office and the National Sound Archive as well as the Social Sciences Library. A subject index is available.
- **The Directory of British Associations CBD Research Ltd** lists brief details of a large number of organisations covering a wide range of subject areas, many of which are very specialised indeed. It has several comparison volumes covering, for example, councils, committees and Boards, European Industrial and trade associations and European professional and learned societies.
- Theses are to be found in *Index to Theses with Abstracts Accepted for Higher Degrees by the Universities of Great Britain and Ireland* (published quarterly).
- Conference Papers are indexed in the British Library Index of Conference Proceedings (published annually).

Libraries and information units should always be approached, in the first instance, by telephone or letter. Let them know concisely the subject of your research, how far you have got with your literature searches and what information you require.

3. Forms of Writing in Social Science

In your work as a social science student you will encounter various forms of writing. For example, there are abstracts, annotations, book reviews and literature reviews – all of which contribute to an understanding and awareness of trends and developments in social science research. These forms of writing serve different functions and this is reflected in their composition and style. In one sense they signify progression from writing which provides a summary of research (an abstract), to writing which has a deeper, analytical and comparative function (book reviews and literature reviews). This chapter aims to enhance your familiarity with these different forms which you will encounter in connection with your own research, before the main forms of undergraduate writing assignments, i.e. essays, are analysed in Chapters Four and Five. This will put you in a stronger position to organise and develop your own writing in these different contexts, as well as enabling you to evaluate the quality of the work of other students and professional writers.

SUMMARY WRITING

The main forms of social science research summaries are abstracts and annotations. Abstracts are summaries of research that usually appear at the beginning of a paper, journal article or book. They provide a useful, quick reference which enables the reader to gain an overview of the research and in many cases to decide whether or not to go on to read the original work. Annotations of other people's research may appear in bibliographies, and provide the reader with brief information beyond that contained in the title.

Writing Your Own Summary

As you prepare your own summary (whether for your own study purposes or as part of a course-work assignment), remember that it will be useful only if it translates, as accurately as possible, many words into few. More than any form of social science writing, abstracts and other summaries require succinct language and precise usage. You will notice in the professional journals with which you are familiar, that length and style are carefully circumscribed to provide a framework of requirements within which the writer must work. If you are summarising as part of your own work and study, you will, of course, have more flexibility, except that you must remember that the whole point of the summary is to write in condensed form, without losing the essential meaning.

To write an effective abstract or a particular annotation, therefore, you must be able to identify the main ideas in a piece of research, to recognise the relevance of these ideas for a particular audience and to organise them clearly and concisely. Although there is no standard formula available, you may find it useful to consider the following points when preparing summaries:

- **What question is posed by this work?** This should be the central concern guiding all your reading of social science literature. In a research report or journal article, the question is usually phrased in terms of some hypothesis or set of hypotheses which outline the relationship between a set of variables. For example, 'it was considered possible that women and men who had been through the selection process required to obtain good mathematics qualifications at school might show similarities in attitude. However, it was also considered possible that the somewhat competitive and impersonal nature of university education might affect women negatively, therefore leading to gender differences of the type found in previous research' (Fraser, 1994).

- **What is the main method of data collection and analysis?** What is the dominant research orientation, e.g., qualitative or quantitative? Were interviews used? Were field observations made? What previous studies were reviewed? When and where was the research conducted? Answers to these questions help to contextualise the work within a wider field and will help in making comparisons with other research.
- **What are the findings?** Given the hypotheses to be tested, what did the researchers discover and what significance attaches to these results? It is sometimes difficult to construct a succinct statement of the findings, particularly if the work you are summarising is a lengthy book. It will help to identify the main focus or thesis because this is something which the findings should address.

Overall, don't hesitate to follow the organisation of the work being summarised. For example, the chapter headings of a book or the standard format of research writing (introduction, methods, results, analysis) can provide a useful framework for your summary. This works particularly well if the author's argument is logically and clearly presented. If not, you may need to develop your own outline. Whatever approach you follow you should aim to introduce the main idea or thesis of the work you are summarising very early on, i.e. in your first or second sentence. **Remember, the main purpose is to report objectively, accurately and briefly; the summary is not the occasion for lengthy comments or analysis of the original material.**

Examples

Abstract

Marshall, G and Swift, A. (1993) 'Social class and social justice', *British Journal of Sociology* 44, 2, p. 187-211. This paper poses the issue of distributive justice in terms of the relationship between social class, social mobility and educational attainment in contemporary Britain. Having discussed various conceptions of justice which might vindicate class inequality, the authors investigate empirically the specifically meritocratic defence, and report survey data suggesting that the effect of class origins on class destinations is only partially mediated by educational achievement. Class privilege can compensate for educational failure. Gender is also significant since women tend to fare worse than men with similiar class origins and credentials. This evidence undermines the claim that Britain is a meritocratic society and supports the suggestion that only by political intervention can equality of opportunity be rendered compatible with significant and structured inequality of outcome.

Annotated bibliography

Bulmer, M. (1982) <u>The Uses of Social Research</u>. London: Allen and Unwin.

An important book which reviews the development of applied social research in Britain and evaluates its potential. Case studies are used to illustrate key themes, including a case study of research on deprivation and disadvantage. There is a good discussion of the institutional context of social research and its implications and also of the engineering and enlightenment models of research. However, the book reflects the dominant tradition of policy-orientated research, and the contribution of qualitative methods is not specifically discussed.

ACTIVITY: WRITING A SUMMARY

Together with one of your fellow students select an article from your current reading list. Write a summary (independently of each other) observing the points of the discussion, as above. Be brief and direct. Exchange summaries and discuss your writing, identifying some of the difficulties and ways in which these could be resolved.

BOOKS REVIEWS

Unlike summaries, book reviews usually reveal what a writer thinks about a particular work – i.e. they include evaluation. In moving beyond the objectivity of the summary statement, the review provides a forum for the writer's voice, while at the same time providing an important research service for social scientists. Book reviews are usually written fairly soon after a book is published allowing researchers to keep up to date with new developments in their field; and because they are brief, they provide a valuable guide to those conducting library research. A good review will offer a cogent summary of the work, indicate its strengths and weaknesses, and assess its contribution to the established literature, together with its implications for further research and development.

As with all types of writing in social sciences a book review is written for a specific audience. Knowing who is most likely to read what we have written will influence the style and content of what we write. In all your course-related writing you should maintain a clear sense of your audience. Remember that you are writing for an 'academic' audience that values well-supported argument and analysis, rather than unsubstantiated assertion, and a demonstrable understanding of significant research in the field of study. (These questions are considered in Chapters Four and Five.)

One method of developing an appropriate style is to examine the different forms of specialist writing available. Book reviews, for example, are included in most of the leading journals and are well worth your consideration. Written by specialists for specialists in the various disciplines of social science, the reviews are based on the assumption that readers are knowledgeable and experienced in the field. Reading and studying such work is valuable both at a content level (i.e. you enhance your stock of knowledge) and at a process level (i.e. you learn how to present ideas in 'academic' form). Other reviews, such as those appearing in newspapers or magazines, will normally be more general in approach, making fewer specialist demands on their readers and providing more description than academic analysis.

Writing a Book Review

As with other forms of writing, a successful book review cannot be accomplished by prescription, but the following points will provide you with a foundation to begin this writing task:

- Be selective, rather than attempting to cover everything in the book. Obviously you will want to give your reader(s) a sense of the entire work, but aim to do this in one or two paragraphs, using your summarising skills. Organise the review around the book's stated objectives or thesis. Avoid working solidly through each item in the table of contents by concentrating on what *you* consider to be important and significant.
- Support your arguments with evidence from the book, using examples that provide ready illustrations of the points you wish to make. Generally, use your own words, in ways which are consistent with the original text. Direct quotations should be avoided, except where you wish to discuss the book's style, lucidity or expressive quality.
- Review the book as it appears, rather than the one which you think the author should have written. Identify the author's main intentions and judge the work on this basis.
- Avoid using the review as an opportunity to ride your own particular 'hobby horse'. Remember, the purpose of the review is to evaluate what the author has written and not to present a discourse on your own (idiosyncratic) beliefs and opinions. Beyond this, and so long as you maintain a critical perspective, you need not feel unduly constrained. You should be encouraged by the words of the contemporary American writer Jon Updike who advised, 'Do not imagine yourself a caretaker of any tradition, an enforcer of any standards, a warrior in any ideological battle, a corrections officer of any kind. Review the book, not the reputation.'

Organising Your Book Review

For a short review of some 500-1,000 words, the following guidelines developed by Barnet and Stubbs (1990) provide a useful approach:

- Start with an introductory paragraph which identifies the work and its author, presents the thesis or main aim of the book and gives some indication of whether the author achieves her/his stated purpose.

- Next, in a paragraph or two summarise the book's main contents; try to relate these, where possible, to other books/research in the field.
- Devote one paragraph to an evaluation of the book, noting its strengths and weaknesses. Try to integrate these so that your approach is as coherent as possible.
- The concluding paragraph(s) should provide an evaluation of the strengths and weaknesses of the book. Does it succeed in answering the questions it poses? The extent of its implications for further research and investigation should be briefly considered.

REVIEW ESSAYS

A variation of this form of social science writing is the review essay. These are critical reviews of books, written by experts in a particular field of study. They are longer than the usual review and devote more time to an assessment of the work within an established research tradition. (Often they will include citations or references to related works.) Review essays provide a forum for the reviewer to engage in a dialogue with the author. The review usually comprises substantial analysis during which a particular line of argument or viewpoint is put forward and supported by relevant evidence. Review essays can provide valuable insights and commentary on issues and controversies within contemporary fields of knowledge and established subject areas. They are well worth consulting and can provide you with important models for your own study and writing activities.

Examples

Reprinted below are two reviews of David Rothman's *The Discovery of the Asylum*. The first was written by an American college student; the second was written by an historian and appeared in a professional journal. The differences in qualifications of the reviewers, and in the audiences for whom they are writing, should be clear as you read and compare these reviews.

Student review: Elizabeth Stone

An examination of asylums
The Discovery of the Asylum by David Rothman is a thought-provoking analysis of the origin and evolution of American institutions. Rothman describes the tumultuous events and public opinion that shaped the way deviants were treated during the eighteenth and nineteenth centuries. Using the perspective of social history, he examines the problems that developed from the decision to isolate society's misfits in asylums.

The book begins with a discussion of the treatment of deviants from the Colonial Period through the Civil War. The colonists believed that deviance was the result of individual weaknesses instead of a flaw in community structure. Workhouses and almshouses were intended to discourage vagrants from invading communities and to house the poor who would "monetarily inconvenience" other residents. But in response to philosophical and practical changes – an emphasis on reason and a growing population – these practices shifted to a desire to "cure" deviants. Now, people began to search for the roots of deviance within society itself. The cure for improper behaviour would be found through a system of rational codes.

It was out of this climate that the institution was born, complete with humanitarian and reformatory goals. The penitentiary, the almshouse, and the asylum were run on the principles of order, discipline, and routine. Rothman describes how ideas for the reform and rehabilitation of deviants were lost and never recovered in the blind concern for the institution's physical organisation and structure. For example, in the prison system, convict labour, lack of parole, and prison crowding eventually turned the asylum into a custodial institution. "The promise of reform had built up the asylums; the functionalism of custody perpetuated them" (240).

This historical account is appealing, largely because of

Rothman's style. He writes with a wry, slightly sarcastic tone, describing the ideas of the time while conveying his personal opinions. To illustrate, consider these words on corporal punishment in orphanages, a practice of which Rothman obviously did not approve: "A good dose of institutionalisation could only work to the child's benefit" (209). The use of frequent quotations reinforces his historical perspective and paints a vivid picture of early American asylums. Unfortunately, Rothman fails to discuss anti-institutional movements during this time, and he offers little insight into the institutional experience from the inside. Nevertheless, Rothman's argument is well-documented. He reviews a different institution in each chapter, showing the effect of this asylum on society from its hopeful beginning to its failure.

Despite these minor shortcomings, *The Discovery of the Asylum* tells a fascinating story. These institutions were established not only to show the national government in a favourable light but also to provide a ready alternative for the accelerating disintegration of Colonial order. If we accept Rothman's argument that rehabilitation was merely a secondary consideration in the development of asylums, we must confront the question: Can the goal of curing deviance be meaningfully introduced into these institutions? Rothman's conclusion gives us some hope that such a thing is possible: "We need not remain trapped in inherited answers".

A Professional Review: Gerald Grob

Rothman, David J. 1971. *The Discovery of The Asylum: Social Order and Disorder in The New Republic*. Boston: Little, Brown.

In a book that is simultaneously a work of history and social

criticism, David J. Rothman presents an interpretation of
American society during the first half of the nineteenth
century that is both provocative and disturbing. His thesis,
which is clear and lucid, is relatively simple. By the early
nineteenth century, according to Rothman, the traditional
and stable society of the colonial period had begun to
disintegrate. Aware of the momentous changes that were
taking place, Americans were uncertain as to how they
should meet the challenges of the new order and restore the
social cohesion they deemed so vital to society. Obsessed
with deviant and dependent behavior, they ultimately came
to the conclusion that "to comprehend and control abnormal
behavior promised to be the first step in establishing a new
system for stabilizing the community, for binding citizens
together."

The solution that Americans adopted, writes Rothman,
involved the creation of the "asylum" – an institution that
would reform criminals, juvenile delinquents, poor and indigent
groups, mentally ill persons, and all other deviants whose
abnormal behavior might or did threaten society. The result was
an incredible proliferation of prisons, almshouses, houses of
refuge, and mental hospitals, to cite only a few. Although most
of these institutions abandoned any pretense at rehabilitation
and rapidly degenerated into custodial institutions that served as
"a dumping ground for social undesirables," they survived
because it was easier to incarcerate undesirables that to seek
new and different solutions.

While *The Discovery of the Asylum* will undoubtedly appeal
to many contemporary readers who will share its author's
anti-institutionalism and moral outrage, as a work of
historical scholarship it leaves something to be desired. First, it
indiscriminately confuses institutions that have superficial
resemblances. A mental hospital – whatever its failures and
shortcomings – *did* care for sick individuals, since its patient
population included substantial numbers of cases of general
paresis and senile psychoses (both of which were clearly of

organic origin). To identify jails, almshouses, and mental hospitals as variations of one species is inaccurate, even though they had much in common. Secondly, a comparative approach casts grave doubts over the validity of Rothman's thesis. If confinement in specialized "asylums" was the response of a nation which feared change and saw institutionalization as a means of social control, how then does one explain the fact that these very same institutions (jails, almshouses, mental hospitals) appeared in England and on the continent either earlier or at the very same time as in America? Yet there is little evidence to indicate that the social order in Europe was undergoing the same or a similar process of distintegration. Thirdly, the book is simplistic; it deals with complex social processes without the subtleties and nuances that mark sophisticated scholarship. Rothman's approach to history is too rationalistic and intellectualized, for he assumes a one-to-one relationship between intent and consequence.

Finally, the evidence used is either incomplete or one-sided. The book in general is not based on manuscript sources, which would have added a dimension that is presently lacking. To write about mental hospitals and yet not to examine the extensive and rich collections of Dorothea L. Dix, Thomas S. Kirkbride, Samuel B. Woodward, Pliny Earle, Edward Jarvis, and others, is unforgivable. Moreover, Rothman has conveniently summarized all of the evidence that validates his thesis, but has neglected or slighted the material that contradicts his interpretation.

I am sorry to be so critical of this book, which despite its defects has many shrewd and brilliant insights. Had Rothamn not been so intent on reducing all phenomena to one simple thesis and offering a lesson to our own generation, his book could have been a major contribution to American social history. That it is not is partly a product of the confusion of ideology with scholarship.

Gerald N. Grob
Rutgers University

LITERATURE REVIEWS

Before beginning investigations of their own, social science researchers need to find out what others in their field have discovered. In this way new research provides a link with the past, while at the same time pointing to new directions for the future. This is achieved by seeking answers to questions that have yet to be asked and challenging answers that form the basis of current, conventional wisdom.

Wanting to know what others have found out provides a powerful reason for professional and student researchers alike to conduct a review of the literature. A review can remain as an independent piece of writing in its own right, or it may well be part of an extended essay or dissertation. As an undergraduate student, it is likely that you will be required to produce a literature review in both contexts. As with other forms of writing, quality and effectiveness are heavily dependent upon an ability to summarise the work of others. However, it is probably fair to say that literature reviews demand more of their writers than other forms of writing. They involve a familiarity with a larger quantity of research and require more exacting skills of selection, classification and critical analysis. In many ways literature reviews are exercises in comparative writing.

Because authors of literature reviews set out to make valid comparisons among a number of related studies, they necessarily pay careful attention to the considerable variations which characterise social science research. Sometimes, it appears that similar studies arrive at contradictory conclusions; however, closer examination reveals that this is because the same concept has been measured in different ways. For example, an American survey on poverty found that poverty was measured by determining the number of people living in sub-standard economic conditions (Williamson and Hyer, 1975). Variations in the financial figures which defined poverty levels was one obvious explanation of the different results, but a number of other factors also influenced the research findings. Did the authors consider individual or family income? Was data collected in a single year or over a period of years? Were forms of public subsistence included in the calculation of welfare status?

This is just one illustration of research sharing **nominal definitions** of a concept, in this case, poverty, but relying on different **operational definitions**, that is, ways of measuring 'poverty'.

Study Variables

Making valid comparisons in a literature review requires not only close scrutiny of how concepts are measured but also attention to many of the technical aspects of social research, for example, variables which have been considered in a particular study. **Dependent variables** represent the main focus of research investigations; they denote sets of attributes which are thought to be caused by the **independent variables**. Given the simple hypothesis, **income varies directly with education**, the dependent variable is '**income**' and '**education**' is the independent variable. In other words, the more education a person has had, the higher his or her income would be expected to be.

If a dependent variable is in fact affected by one or more independent variables, manipulating the independent variables should result in a change in the dependent variable. If researchers were concerned, for example, that the effect of education on income might be influenced according to whether a person was black or white, they might introduce race as a **control variable**.

Generally, control variables pose the question: given the presence of control variable R, does the relationship between X (an independent variable) and Y (a dependent variable) change? In this example, as you would expect, introducing race as a control would involve comparing the relationship between education and income for whites, with the same relationship for blacks. It is important to pay particular attention to the use of **dependent** and **control variables** and the ways in which they shape and qualify general research questions.

As you prepare your literature review, you will inevitably refer to many different studies and you will need to decide on the information you require and how this is to be collected and used. Methods of summarising and evaluating the findings of each relevant study or research project, prior to the task of synthesis and incorporation into a larger literature review are described below.

CONSTRUCTING REVIEW ENTRIES

Each potential contribution to your literature review should be organised as follows:

- **Record the complete bibliographic reference** of the work you are reviewing. This should be completed as you proceed on a separate index card, and should be done in a standard form which you use throughout your work. For example, 'Bauman, Z. (1992) Intimations of PostModernity. London: Routledge'. This can save hours of effort later on trying to trace a particular reference.
- **Identify the major questions** which have been addressed. Where possible state the main ideas of the research hypothesis as specifically as you can but in your own words. This will help sort out your ideas and avoid problems with paraphrasing and summarising at a later stage.
- **Define the method of investigation** (for empirical research studies). Determine whether qualitative or quantitative techniques have been used (these approaches are discussed more fully in Chapter Five) and the ways in which they have been used. Describe modes of observation, e.g. questionnaires, personal interviews, archival searches. Note the time scale for the study if one is stated.
- **Identify the major variables and their operational definitions.** You will recall, from the discussion above, that the way in which concepts are defined influences the results as well as the implications of a piece of research. Record how each variable is measured and where possible, identify dependent, independent and control variables.
- **Describe the study population.** How is the sample defined? Does it comprise individuals, groups or organisations or collections of artefacts, e.g. newspapers, television commercials or magazine advertisements. Was a method of sample selection used in selecting the group? Give particular attention to any differences which developed within the study population, for example, attitudinal differences.
- **State the outcomes of the research in sufficient detail.** Don't just write: '. . . age had a significant effect on voter participation . . .'. Instead give the magnitude and level of the effect, for example: '. . . age was positively correlated with voter participation (r =0.37). This

correlation was statistically significant at the 0.05 level . . .'. Similar care should be taken to note the outcomes of **qualitative studies**. For example, '. . . regardless of their age or race, men were more likely than women to give their unsolicited opinions about the proposed change in club membership policies . . .'.

- **Record the writer's own evaluative comments** separately as they will serve as a basis for analysis in your literature review. You may find that researchers who present similar results reach different conclusions, or you may wish to dispute the interpretation given.
- **Conclude with a personal reflection;** leave a space at the end of each entry to formulate your own response to the work you have considered and its relationship to other research which you have read. Recording your observations in this way should help with the task of organising your different summaries and writing a first draft of your literature review.

ORGANISING THE SUMMARIES

Literature reviews are usually organised either **topically** or **chronologically**; most frequently they are structured **topically**. In such cases previous research is divided into segments representing conceptual subsets of some larger issue. For example, a review of a concept like alienation, which has identifiable dimensions, may be logically organised in the light of these dimensions, i.e., powerlessness, meaninglessness, or normlessness.

Similarly, reviews of a particular institution, such as the criminal courts, may be organised according to different methodologies through which they have been studied. If you are interested in judicial sentencing, for example, you may find that it makes sense to separate entries for your review into qualitative and quantitative sections. This is especially important where different methodologies have been used to ask different questions. A qualitative approach, such as making field observations in a criminal courtroom, may yield valuable insights, for example, into the dynamics between defendant and judge, but is not always the most appropriate way to proceed. Where the aim is to examine the relationship between a defendant's previous record and sentencing outcomes over a period of 20 years, a more qualitative approach, through an archival search of court documents, is likely to be more feasible in this and similar studies.

The second common way of organising literature is **chronological**. Ordering the entries in your review according to when they were published provides an historical context for your topic. If your goal is to discuss a particular concept, from its emergence to its present use within a discipline, a chronological review is a useful analytical strategy. It reveals which contributions have been the most significant (in terms of repeated reference by others); it points to periods of dormancy during which little work was done on a particular topic, and it identifies changes in theories and methods which characterise the development of academic disciplines.

It also makes good sense to organise a review chronologically if you wish to follow the development of social science research alongside historical developments occurring outside its boundaries. Consider, for example, research on race relations in post-war Britain, and in particular research on Commonwealth Immigration, an area of enormous controversy and conflict. This post-war debate can be studied using various perspectives. To take just one , the legislative framework established with the passing of the Nationality Act in 1948 (reinforced by further acts in 1962, 1968 and 1971, before its completion in 1981 with a New Nationality Act), it is possible to chart powerful changes in social policy and community attitudes in which citizenship rights of Afro-Caribbean and Asian people have been systematically eroded and removed. The early research, which investigated the adaptive processes facing immigrants in their new circumstances (Patterson 1965) has long since given way to more politicised studies seeking to illuminate and address the politics and concepts of racism (Gilroy, 1987; Husband, 1982; Miles, 1989).

Using an historical framework for the review of such topics can help you trace the currents of social change as they emerge and are manifested in social science research. This type of chronology can dramatically illustrate the force with which history shapes what social scientists consider worth knowing, as well as demonstrating the ways in which they acquire knowledge.

DRAFTING YOUR REVIEW

The way in which summaries are prepared and organised will be fundamentally influenced by the aims of the review. Usually your literature review will form part of an extended essay or dissertation but you may be asked to write a more free-standing review based upon a particular theme or topic. Additionally, in shorter pieces of writing that you undertake, for example, your essays, you will need to refer to relevant literature to support your argument and to illustrate the points you make, although in a less extensive way.

When you undertake a major literature review, you will collect different entries that summarise the purpose of research, and various dimensions, including methods, operationalisation of major concepts, observations from different populations, and discrepancies in findings which provide you with a basis for comparison. The number of comparisons you could address is potentially large, so how do you go about constructing your argument?

Let us assume that you want to compare a number of studies concerned with the same hypotheses but which differ in their findings. One way of proceeding is first to discuss each piece of research in turn, and then conclude by attempting to account for the discrepancies in outcome among them. This is an effective method if the number of entries in the review is relatively small. However, when you are reviewing one large body of research, and in order to avoid an approach in which studies are simply 'catalogued' rather than critically reviewed, it is important to be **selective**, by referring to one or two substantial studies which represent broadly supported findings. For instance, you might write that:

> 'Robertson's (1972) analysis of crime in Atlanta showed that most thefts are never reported to the police.'

After describing this principle entry, you could add that:

> 'Smith (1983), McFarland (1966), and Jones (1985) report similar findings in their investigations of other American cities.'

Finally, limit your description of each study to the essential elements which will be used in the comparison. Provide enough information about the research to sustain **analysis**, but do not yield to the temptation to give long **descriptive** passages of each work. Research findings do not all deserve equal attention in your review. Work will vary in importance and significance and you should aim to give more detailed attention to the 'landmark' studies that inspire many others.

A Plan for Your Literature Review

In preparing your literature review, your planning outline might be as follows:

- Statement of thesis; purpose and focus of the review.
- Literature reviewed; analysis of relevant studies.
- Comparative analysis; points of similarity and difference.
- Conclusion or summary analysis; explanation of points of comparison or contrast.

An alternative strategy is to begin describing the characteristics of research shared by several studies, and then to move to an analysis of their differences. This approach has the advantage of easily conforming to a 'topical structure' because the generic aspects of the research – the findings, methods, and so forth – guide your analysis, rather than the discrete research investigations themselves. An alternative outline might be as follows:

- Statement of thesis.
- Similarities in the research.
- Differences in the research.
- Conclusion.

Whatever type of comparative analysis you adopt, you must guide your readers through the review beginning with a strong statement of intent. Let them know exactly how the review is to be organised and what your analytical strategy will be. If appropriate, specify the historical period covered in your review. Defining your terms in this way at the outset may deflect criticism that you have failed to consider the literature relevant to your topic.

Beginning Your Review

The following introduction to a review of the literature on sex roles should provide you with some ideas on starting.

Example: Introduction to a Literature Review

> Hundreds of studies have addressed sex-role differentiation, but the findings have not been systematically integrated to form a cumulative body of knowledge. Our understanding of the processes by which sex roles influence the system of social stratification is especially limited. We add our review to those of others (e.g. Lipman-Blumen and Tickamyer 1975; Pleck 1977; Waite and Hudis 1980; Scanzoni and Fox 1980) in order to further this synthesis, identifying critical theoretical questions and effective research strategies.
>
> In this paper we examine recent literature on the sexual division of labor. We are particularly concerned with sex roles as fundamental channeling and integrative mechanisms. The review focuses on two major areas: the division of labor in the family and in the economy. Although they are obviously interrelated, we first address sexual differentiation in each realm separately before considering sex roles as an integrating mechanism coordinating work and family roles (Miller and Garrison 1982, p. 237).

Follow your introductory remarks by using 'signposts' to guide your reader through the main stages of your review. Use short section titles or strong transitional sentences to signify moving from one study or issue to another. If the review is necessarily and unavoidably long, it is sometimes a good idea to include intermediate summaries. As you conclude your review, make sure that you:

- Go beyond a simple summary statement.
- Give your own interpretations, supported by relevant evidence.

- Summarise questions which have been addressed and those left unanswered.
- Identify the more important and significant works you have encountered, and say *why* they are important and significant.
- Indicate areas for future investigation and research.

Remember that an effective literature review not only reveals what social scientists have done, it also serves as the foundation for future work.

4. Student Assignments

Your course of undergraduate study in social science is likely to involve some three years full-time study or five years (even longer under certain conditions) of part-time study. During this period you will be called upon to produce various assignments, most of which, it has to be said, will be written. The context of writing will vary, but the usual form will be the essay, a writing assignment which generally comprises some 2,000-4000 words. This 'short form' essay is the main focus of this chapter, although other forms – for example, writing in support of oral presentations and writing under examination conditions – are considered.

ESSAY WRITING

The essay is a standard form of writing for most students in social sciences. Usually they are:

- Required at regular intervals, that is, there is no escape!
- Set in advance at the beginning of the module or course of study, i.e. there is time for planning, drafting and rewriting.
- Based upon secondary (i.e. library-based research) rather than primary data produced as a result of individual investigative field research.
- Assessed as part of coursework, hence are critical to your work and progress.

AN INTERACTIVE PROCESS

Writing an essay is not simply a matter of 'writing'. Essentially you are engaged in an interactive process that alternates and combines writing with research activity. Once your assignment has been set and your task and responsibility is known to you, it will be necessary to think about your approach and what information you may require. Alternatively, if you are able to choose your own topic, you will gain ideas for writing from a variety of sources including discussions in your lectures or seminar groups or as a result of your reading. Whatever the source, it is likely that you will begin your information search at an early stage and begin to make notes, from the outset, on what you discover to be potentially relevant and interesting. This will help you to focus your thoughts and develop a shape and perspective for your topic.

Following this early work, you should be clearer about your project and thus be able to return to the library feeling confident to undertake a more directed and focused information-gathering and note-taking exercise. At this stage you will begin to read material in a new way, testing ideas that you are beginning to form about the topic. When you incorporate these new themes into your essay, you may find that your focus has changed in a significant way and hence it is necessary to reformulate the organisation and structure of your paper.

The main point is that you do not simply go to the library, collect all the books and journals that you need, or that you think you need, and sit down and write. You may have to make several trips to the library in order to clarify and revise your tentative first thoughts about the topic, before you are on your way to writing a coherent paper. All this means that writing an essay takes more time than you may have anticipated, so it is imperative that you get an early start. It is never too soon to begin thinking and jotting down notes, recording ideas and thoughts and reflecting on your reading. As you engage in this interactive process you are beginning to develop contents for your essay, some of which will appear in your final version.

DIFFERENT FORMS OF ESSAY

Essays can take various forms. For example, they may be open-ended assignments in which you have some scope for selecting your own subject. If this is the case there are several ways you can proceed. For example, you could choose:

- A current event or public issue(s) to describe and analyse within a general explanatory framework, e.g. child abuse – patterns of socialisation and pathologies; the national curriculum – influences of the 'new right' in education policy development.
- A comparative analysis focusing on two or three subsets of some general phenomenon, e.g. gender as a factor in academic performance in young adults; majority and minority religious groups and attitudes towards abortion.

As even these few examples illustrate, the range of possible subjects about which you might write is immense. This is one of the attractions of writing about social science, but there is a risk in being too general and detached from a relevant theoretical framework. The first step in writing a good, high quality essay is to narrow the range of possible subjects into a clear, manageable focus.

CHOOSING A TOPIC

How do you go about selecting a topic for an essay? During your programme of study new units and courses will present you with a large number of interesting questions, but obviously not all of them can be developed into an effective essay or paper, however strong your interest might be. Even when the title or topic is set by your tutor, you are still presented with a number of problems in making out a coherent and well researched paper.

As you develop ideas about a topic, ask yourself the following questions:

- **Is the topic relevant to the course or module of study for which it is a required assignment?** For example, you might write about the causes of crime for both a psychology and a sociology course, but the focus of the two papers will differ considerably. Psychologically, you might investigate individual pathologies and the causality of violent crime. A sociological study is not reducible to such individual factors as it is concerned with human relationships, exchanges and dependencies. The focus of study might be to explain why and under what circumstances particular groups of people associate for criminal purposes and form distinctive sub-cultures. When you begin to research an essay topic, check your course notes and reading list to clarify the areas to be covered in lectures and seminars and build from this basis. If you have any doubts about the relevance of your chosen subject and the perspective(s) you envisage using, consult your tutor as early as possible.

- **Is the topic researchable?** You may be particularly interested in a topic only to discover that there is a paucity of information and research available. For example, some areas of current interest have not yet made their way into the published literature; other topics may be plagued by methodological difficulties, such as problems of access or confidentiality. This does not mean that you should limit your choice of work to areas with a voluminous literature but some clear thinking will be necessary in order to select an appropriate topic.

- **Is my topic interesting?** While you should always strive to select a topic that will be interesting to your readers, you should attempt, above all, to select one that interests you, despite the routine of producing considerable numbers of essays over the period of your studies. If you become bored with a topic, you can be sure that your lack of interest will carry over to your writing.

- **Is my topic clearly defined?** One of the most difficult processes in developing an essay is narrowing down the subject into a workable content area which is consistent with the specification of the essay you have been set. This will not happen at once but from an initial general stage it will be possible to focus on a more specific approach.

ORGANISING YOUR ESSAY

Clear and logical organisation is essential to writing an effective essay. Once you have determined the form your argument will take, you have made considerable progress. At this point, and as you begin to reflect on the substance of your essay, you should allocate a sufficient time for thinking about how to put the various different aspects together.

The organisation of your paper will be guided to some extent by your subject. For example, if you are writing about a specific event or issue, some discussion is necessary before proceeding with the analysis. If you are comparing two or three instances of some phenomenon (e.g. three alternative educational programmes) you might begin by briefly describing each and then going on to discuss their similarities and differences. If your topic is a concept rather than a particular event, you might write about it in terms of different aspects, discussing each of these in turn. A paper on the socio-psychological effects of divorce, for instance, might be divided into sections that discuss the effects of the divorce on children, family members and friends.

DEVELOPING THE ANALYSIS

As you consult different theoretical and empirical writings, perhaps drawing further upon additional library sources, and you begin to reflect, reject and draw contents together, you are engaging in a process of analysis. However, it is important to emphasise that your analysis can only succeed if you have already established categories into which your contents can be placed.

You must not (and this is a common error, particularly among first-year students) simply collect 'library information' and then describe and discuss your 'findings' in some notional order, for example, as you have located them! Instead, you must first decide upon a method or rationale for categorising the different information, views and arguments which you have collected. Among other things, this will enable you to decide that one particular study should be mentioned first, another last, while another piece of research may not be included at all.

As you make these kinds of decisions, you are forced to examine the interrelationships between the different parts that together can support your overall thesis or argument, and which constitute your completed essay. To some extent, because you are relying on secondary source materials, you are constrained by what others have done. Remember, though, that you are responsible for evaluating and organising the material in a way that supports your argument, and for providing explanations for that which does not.

OUTLINING

A useful way to construct the categories you use, is to develop an outline or plan of your intended essay. This is particularly appropriate if the assignment involves secondary or library-based research as it will help you to distinguish between major and minor issues, to collect relevant data and information and to identify additional material you may need. In setting out the main themes in this way you reduce the risk of being repetitive. The example below is taken from an essay which analysed a specific case of corporate misconduct in the United States and the charges of misleading advertising brought by the Federal Trade Commission (FTC) against Warner-Lambert, the manufacturer of *Listerine*. The initial outline was envisaged as follows:

- Background of *Listerine* case.
- Legal aspects – FTC v Warner-Lambert.
- Sociological issues raised by the case.

This provided a basis upon which a more detailed outline could be developed following further, library-based research and a critical consideration of further relevant materials. A more developed outline is as follows:

Background of Listerine Case
- FDA drug efficacy study (*New York Times* 1969)
- Focus on mouthwash producers (*New York Times* 1970)

The Case – Federal Trade Commission v Warner-Lambert Co. (Trade Regulations Reports)
- Notification and issuance of the complaint
- Administrative hearing before FTC
- Final order to cease and desist
- Appeals – U.S. Court and Supreme Court

Sociological issues
- Nature and structure of the case
  - administrative v criminal law
  - difficulty of establishing intent
- Normative dimensions of the case
  - ambiguity of norms governing advertising
  - consumers as victims
- Enforcement of the norms
  - problems in judicial interpretation
  - overlapping jurisdiction of control agents
  - organisational stigma

Effects of the Case
- On Warner-Lambert
- On the advertising community

Having reached this stage in the development of the outline, the next step should be to confirm the literature references that underpin each different section so that your writing can progress within a framework that has some structure. It is important to recognise that this is also flexible and, remembering the importance of creativity discussed in Chapter One, that the organisation and content may be changed as writing develops during a second draft. The outline thus provides a sense of direction and a provisional arrangement of content. You should note, however, the following cautionary points:

- **Do not substitute outlining for actually beginning writing.** You can easily spend hours constructing one outline after another and revising the different elements within it, without necessarily writing a better paper as a result.
- **Resist the temptation to keep planning.** Sometimes, you will know what you have to say only after you begin to write your paper (see comments in Chapter One).
- **Use the outline as a guide, not a prescription for your writing.** If, as you write, it makes sense to stray from the outline from time to time, then do so. If, on the other hand, your paper bears little resemblance to the outline, make sure that your essay still tells a logical and coherent story; as a test, try outlining it!

PLANNING – ANOTHER FORM

Your approach to writing your assignment will inevitably involve some form of planning, but you may feel that outlining provides you with a list of headings at the expense of a deeper sense of relationship between the different areas. You should aim to 'write your way' into your essay. The example below, based upon an essay dealing with tourism and the implications for culture and identity, illustrates how the processes of writing and thinking about concepts and theories begin to merge, to produce a preliminary statement that is perceptive and distinctive.

> **Essay title: 'In the past we had travel, today we have tourism'. – A critique.**
>
> **Background**
> • **two main strands:**
> **Tourism today** – what does it involve? What are the dynamics of negotiating a tourist attraction? What is a 'tourist attraction', and how do people of diverse cultural backgrounds come to recognise it as such?
> **Travel in the past** – what did this involve? Early forms of leisure travel were confined to the aristocracy. Young aristocrats were sent on 'Grand Tours'. The expansion of their literacy and linguistic understanding provided a way of enhancing their social status within upper class society.

What follows from this?

- Notions of seeing, searching and attaching value to specific sights generated a rejection of past intellectual practices; the emphasis shifted from the written word to the 'image'.

- Simultaneous advancement in travel and the realisation that labour could be made more productive through regulated leisure, hastened the advent of annual holidays. From modest beginnings, travel in England and later in Europe, was no longer an elitist activity. Business entrepreneurs, e.g. *Thomas Cook*, quickly realised the potential. Travel as a service industry developed and boomed with the 'package holiday'.

- As the novelty of travel disappears we seek other gratifications, we search for the authentic – we try to glimpse what those around us have failed to notice.

- Notions of the authentic become intrinsic and crucial in advertising holidays – 'see the real Greece'. What we are being offered is the 'unique', individual experience. Holiday companies offer to seek out the authentic and to signify it as such on our behalf. As Culler points out, ' constrained by our cultural identities, it is only through these reproductions that we, as tourists, are able to glimpse the authentic'.

- Constrained as we are by our cultural values, we are forced to put some form of mediator between us and the 'other' culture; the tour guide is just such a mediator. The guide acts not as a pathfinder but as someone to thread one sight with the next, to provide a complete and coherent 'picture' of the cultural importance of the place. In a sense the guide constructs an interpretive framework for the tourist, enabling them to share his sense of the place's significance (Bowman).

- The tourist is only able to engage with 'markers' of the 'authentic', rather than to form a more direct relationship with it. 'We go not to test the image by reality, but to test reality by the image'. (Boorstin).

- The traveller of the past is actively searching for new lands and peoples and thus more directly engages with other cultures. Tourists are passive, they expect interesting things to happen to them. Modern travel, through technology, is de-sensitised and removed from the landscape – there is no sense of accumulating experiences *en route* (Boorstin).

Summary Analysis/Conclusion
- Modern travel limits the contact that can be made with other cultures. In the past, we had to work at travelling; today we merely arrive. The dynamics of the way we engage with other cultures, both past and present, remains the same; it is more a question of varying degrees of engagement, than of different forms.

- The notions of the 'marked attraction' or 'pseudo event', are such complete and international phenomena that it is impossible for the modern traveller to do anything but participate in them. Constrained by our own cultural identities we need these markers or staged events as a means of interpretation, albeit that they provide a watered down, sanitised glimpse of other cultures; without them we would not have a basis to see anything beyond our own cultural experience.

This discursive method can provide excellent ideas and higher level conceptual frameworks at an early stage. At the same time it risks the omission of relevant content, repetition and the poor organisation of undifferentiated text. Not an approach for faint hearts!

ACTIVITY: OUTLINE YOUR NEXT ESSAY

- After you have spent some time researching your topic, sketch a broad outline that includes the key points/themes that you will cover in your essay.
- Continue your research, review your initial outline and develop more detail by adding sub-headings under each major heading.
- Discuss and evaluate your outline.

BALANCE

The elements of good writing are proportional to one another in such a way that the paper as a whole appears to be of uniform design and scale. A paper which lacks balance can cause the reader to lose sight of the author's main intentions. Try to achieve a balance between:

- **Quotation and summary.** Try not to overquote; summarising the work of others is usually a more effective strategy than direct quotation.
- **Description and analysis.** You should not spend much time describing something unless you plan to use the description in your analysis. Your tutors are primarily interested in your ability to analyse an event, institution or other social phenomenon. Lengthy descriptions of particular events or of published research add nothing of substance or significance to your essay; they must be supplemented by analysis that tells your reader *why* this descriptive material is so important.
- **Sections of the paper.** It is often useful to divide the essay into sections by using sub-headings. As well as providing a guide to the essay, this allows readers (and yourself as writer) to assess the relative strength of descriptive and analytical sections and to evaluate the relationship of the introduction and conclusion to the main study of the work.

Example: A Student Essay

Below is a library-based essay on community-orientated care of the mentally ill written by a first-year student. The strengths of the essay can be summarised as follows:

- The essay is based on a good review of relevant literature (17 sources are included in the reference section).
- The essay is well-organised with a useful introduction and thoughtful conclusion.
- The main focus of the essay is stated early on. By the end of the third paragraph we know that the writer will concentrate on public resistance to community facilities; by the beginning of the fifth paragraph we know she will attempt to explain what factors determine resistance to these facilities by mentally ill people.
- There is a good sense of organisation and structure.
- The writer does not merely summarise each study cited; she inserts her voice into the essay.

- The writer rarely quotes source materials, relying instead upon effective paraphrase to enhance the narrative flow.

Public Reaction
to Community Based Care
for the Mentally Ill

Lindsay Elizabeth Moran
April 1988
Writing 125H

The debate over the most effective method for treating the mentally ill dates back to the early nineteenth century. At that time, the work of Philippe Panal in France and William Tuke in England supported the notion that mental illnesses were organic, hereditary diseases; thus, physicians were the primary caretakers of the mentally ill. In the United States, optimism regarding a cure for mental illness was sustained by Dorothea Dix who was largely responsible for encouraging the establishment of state-supported asylums. By the 1840s asylums were claiming to cure over 90% of their inmates. However, the illusion of cure diminished after the Civil War, and a long period of apathy concerning treatment of the insane ensued. Despite evolving theories of psychology, institutions remained and their conditions deteriorated consistently until the Second World War. It was not until the 1960s that the perpetual failures of institutionalization compelled a transformation in treatment of the insane: deinstitutionalization. The change from hospitals to community-based facilities for the mentally ill has been one of the most significant developments in psychiatric care over the last three decades (Hogan 1986a).

Early in the 1960s, social critics noted that mental hospitals fostered patients' dependence on total institutions and hindered their return to productive roles in society (Goffman 1961). Growing humanitarian concern about the lack of individualized care in mental hospitals led to the establishment of community mental health facilities nationwide. In a review of the literature on the treatment of the chronically mentally ill, Althoff, Anthony, Buell, and Sharrat (1972) concluded that community facilities were the most effective way of enabling patients to function independently. Furthermore, residential group homes provided the fundamental components for reducing recidivism and preventing initial hospitalization: an individualized approach, assistance in meeting basic needs and ongoing – rather than time-limited – care (Test 1981).

All of the new services originating within the deinstitutionalization movement – halfway houses, day and night hospitals, foster homes, outpatient clinics, and group homes – share the common elements of being community oriented and residentially located. Despite research replete with examples of the success of community treatment programs (Althoff et al. 1972; Kiesler 1982; Test 1981), public resistance toward alternative care facilities has been the greatest barrier for the deinstitutionalization movement (Gudeman and Shore 1984). Indeed, there is little question that community acceptance of the chronically mentally ill has declined rather than improved (Cutler 1986). This public resistance has been shown to impede the establishment of community based facilities (Baron and Piasecki 1981; Hogan 1986a), thereby preventing considerable progress in the care of the mentally ill.

When one considers the positive aspects of community care for the mentally ill, it is difficult to imagine that the American public would respond negatively to its advent and implementation. Nevertheless, in 1975, public opposition led to a statewide suspension of California's deinstitutionalization program (Severy, Silvers, and Wilmouth 1987). As many as one-half of all psychiatric facilities planned for residential areas are believed to have been blocked as a result of community intervention (Baron and Piasecki 1981; Hogan 1986a). The American media document and perpetuate the impact of public response with extensive coverage about citizens' protests over an increasing number of mentally ill in their presence.

What is the rationale behind public opposition, and is it, in any way, justifiable? Most researchers agree that community opposition is "a response to a perceived threat to the quality of life in a neighborhood" (Hogan 1986a). In one study (Rabin, Muhlin, and Cohen 1984) telephone surveys in New York City were used to determine the reasons why community members opposed residential facilities for the mentally ill. The most commonly cited problems associated with community based care for the mentally ill were undesirable people in the area, the adverse effect on real estate values, a threat to personal safety, creation of an undesirable neighborhood image, and an increase in local crime. In spite of mental health education efforts, communities are more aware of the exploits of dangerous patients than of those patients who are good citizens (Baron and Piasecki 1981). Steadman (1981) suggests that there is an element of increased risk to a community from ex-mental patients which justifies citizens' fear. His research shows that former mental patients are arrested for violent crimes three times as often as the general public.

Still, arrest statistics are not necessarily a valid indicator of the effects of deinstitutionalization, and it remains unclear as to whether the negative attitudes about the establishment of local psychiatric facilities are based on actual experiences or if they merely reflect unsubstantiated prejudices. Most studies suggest that community reactions are a manifestation of predispositions toward the mentally ill. Survey research in Florida showed that group homes for the mentally ill (as compared with those for the mentally retarded and the elderly) receive the least amount of support from all common groups within a community (Severy et al. 1987). Clearly, the perception that insanity is a crime, rather than an illness, has not been eliminated. Survey research conducted in Canada showed that those who harbor generally unfounded prejudices toward the mentally ill are those most likely to oppose implementation of deinstitutionalized facilities (Dear, Hall, and Taylor 1979). Steadman (1981) maintains that mental patients, as an aggregate, are viewed by the public as dangerous and unpredictable, regardless of their behaviour. The general conclusion that emerges from a review of the research conducted over 25 years is that, while people are better informed about the medical model concept of insanity, attitudes toward the mentally ill remain biased and negative (Rabkin 1974). While there is little empirical evidence to substantiate a link between predispositions about the mentally ill and community opposition, extensive research has been conducted to determine the characteristics of neighborhoods that are most likely to reject residential psychiatric facilities. Research from the late 1970s showed that mental health facilities that enabled the highest levels of integration between the patients and the community were those located in areas having low social cohesion (Segal and Trute 1976). Neighborhoods with a low proportion of married couples, high rates of single parent families or single and divorced individuals, and large populations of older people were least likely to express opposition to the presence of a mental health facility. Significantly, most of these neighborhoods were characterized by low income levels, leading one to wonder if prejudice toward the mentally ill is an attitude distinctive of the more privileged classes. Data from the same study indicated that suburban areas with higher income levels, particularly those with nuclear families and those homogeneous in terms of race, class, and educational background, had little or no social interaction between the patients and the community.

Other studies yielded similar conclusions. Combining data from a survey of sheltered care residences in California with that of census tracts where community facilities are located, Baumohl,. Moyles, and Segal (1980) found that conservative middle class communities were the most likely to exhibit strong negative reactions to the development of group homes for the mentally ill. They determined that these reactions have an extremely harmful effect on the social integration of the patients. Interviews with 499 residents of community-based facilities revealed that when they perceived reactions of the community, they felt alienated, and their social integration was reduced. Conservative, working class neighborhoods had a moderate level of community rejection, while liberal, nontraditional neighborhoods conformed most closely to the idea of accepting neighborhoods.

Characteristics of the facilities and their residents also seem to influence the degree to which communities accept or reject the presence of the mentally ill. The term "community mental health facilities" encompasses a broad range including commercial boarding homes, organized group homes, and outpatient facilities. It is not surprising that those facilities which are not distinguishable from regular houses are the least likely to encounter opposition (Dear et al. 1979). More fundamentally, the visibility of deviant behavior determines reactions to the mentally ill. Bizarre or disruptive behavior, as opposed to withdrawal, provokes more negative reactions (Rabkin 1974).

The most noteworthy finding of research on deinstitutionalization of the mentally ill is that community attitudes seem to be marked by ambiguity. While deinstitutionalization efforts – especially group residential facilities – have consistently met with vehement opposition, survey research of a random sample of Florida residents shows that all groups (in terms of age, occupation, and socioeconomic status) of the general public viewed deinstitutionalization programs more favourably than institutionalization (Severy et al. 1987). With the exception of estate agents, respondents indicated widespread support for community based programs.

In another study, Hogan (1986a) used data describing 171 attempts to locate group homes for mentally ill in New Jersey to see which factors contributed to the intensity of opposition. Not surprisingly, resistance was more intense in upper and middle class neighborhoods. What is surprising, however, is that residents were less likely to express opposition if they learned about an intended facility in their neighborhood less than three months before the patients were scheduled to move in. This implies that if neighbors learn early that a home for the mentally ill is going to be located in their community, they have more time to mobilize and organize opposition, and, thus, are more likely to try to prevent the establishment of a group home if they have a collective spokesman. Community opposition, then, seems to occur only when circumstances facilitate organized resistance.

When examining research showing that neighborhood facilities for the mentally ill do not necessarily constitute a social burden to the community (Dear et al. 1979; Rabkin et al. 1984), the nature of community attitudes is ironically contradictory. One survey in Toronto (Dear et al. 1979) sought, among other things, to assess the relationship between attitudes and intended opposition to existing facilities for the mentally ill. Of 384 persons selected because they lived within one quarter of a mile of an existing facility, only 139 were aware of its presence. Furthermore, of those 139, 102 reported that they were in favor of the facility, 19 were indifferent, and only 18 were opposed. Only five out of the 18 had ever taken an action to oppose the facility.

In the New York City study cited previously, Rabkin et al. (1984) sough to determine the impact of proximity of psychiatric facilities on attitudes toward the mentally ill. Despite the fact that one half of the survey respondents were selected because they were living within one block of a facility, 77% were not aware of its existence. More than 75% of those who were "unaware" said they would not object to having one set up near their home. Only 2% said they would take any action to have it moved elsewhere. Oddly, of those selected because they did not live in the vicinity of a mental facility, 13% incorrectly reported the presence of one. Among those who reported (correctly or not) the presence of a home for the mentally ill, 54% said that they had no opposition to it, and most regarded its impact on the community as "negligible". All respondents were asked whether they thought mental patients treated in the community are a danger to people in the area. An overwhelming 74% said "No," while 15% responded "Yes," and 11% were "Uncertain". This led the researchers to conclude that experience was not a determinant of attitudes concerning the danger of mental patients. Even in a community immediately adjacent to a large outpatient psychiatric facility, "crazy people in the streets" were less of a concern than nine other hypothetical community problems presented to the respondents. The most striking finding of Rabkin et al. (1984), as in the Toronto study, is commonly members' unawareness of a nearby facility for the mentally ill.

If community attitudes are, in fact, more favorable than commonly supposed, and opposition is limited to a vocal minority whose views do not represent the community as a whole, the high percentage of residential facilities which are prevented due to neighborhood intervention is not explained. In both studies, it may be that many of the responses could be discredited because people are less likely to report negative reactions toward the mentally ill in an interview situation.

Undeniably, public resistance is a prominent barrier to deinstitutionalization, the impact of which deserves recognition. Negative attitudes have a profoundly deleterious effect on the social integration of residents in community care (Baumohl et al. 1980). In addition, the growth of community facilities for the chronically mentally ill has not kept pace with the recognized need, and there is now a growing population of homeless mentally ill (Gudeman and Shore 1984). Elpers (1987) argues that this will lead to another trend toward institutionalization, as more and more homeless are taken off the streets and placed in psychiatric hospitals or asylums. While no one seemed to realize, during the initial stages of deinstitutionalization, that increased contact between the mentally ill and members of the community might engender friction, Rabkin (1974, p. 305) cautions that "if the force of public opinion is not taken into account, the eventual outcome may be exacerbation of public fear accompanied by a retreat to custodial care and removal from the community".

If the present trend is indeed toward institutionalization of the mentally ill (Elpers 1987), members of the mental health profession must devise a method for overcoming community opposition so that community treatment is not seen as a failure. Otherwise, community treatment will only serve to perpetuate the stigma of the mentally ill and foster an aura of hopelessness about their care. Hogan (1986b) suggests utilizing public relations strategies that appear effective in gaining support for group home locations, such as obtaining support from local government and increasing community involvement with the patients. The research of Dear et al. (1979) showed that increased interaction between members of the community and residents of facilities does foster tolerance toward the mentally ill. However, these researchers maintain that mental health professionals need to acknowledge, to a greater extent, that the public's perception of threat or danger from mental health patients has some validity. Perceived danger and fear is the essence of the stigma, and these will proliferate if people consider them to be general societal attitudes. The media could make a positive contribution by not over-emphasizing the reaction of certain community members to the mentally ill.

Since the implementation of deinstitutionalization policies, identification and understanding of public attitudes toward the mentally ill has assumed a new significance. With the growing population of homeless mentally ill, the challenge for community residences of the mentally ill appears even greater today that at their inception. There is a need to continue educating communities about the realities of treating chronic mental patients in facilities outside of hospitals. These realities, both positive and negative, must be accepted by all factions of society if we are to stop the cycle of failure that has become characteristic of treatment for the mentally ill.

References

Althoff, Michael, William Anthony, Gregory Buell, and Sara Sharrat. 1972. "Efficacy of Psychiatric Rehabilitation." Psychological Bulletin 78: 447-456.

Baron, R., and J. Piasecki, 1981. "The Community Versus Community Care." Pp. 63-76 in New Directions for Mental Health Services: Issues in Community Residential Care, edited by R. Budson. San Francisco: Jossey-Bass.

Baumohl, Jim, Edwin Moyles, and Steven Segal. 1980. "Neighborhood Types and Community Reaction to the Mentally Ill: A Paradox of Intensity." Journal of Health and Social Behaviour 21: 345-359

Cutler, David L. 1986. "Community Residential Options for the Chronically Mentally Ill." Community Mental Health Journal 22: 61-73.

Dear, M., G. Hall, and S.Taylor. 1979. "Attitudes Toward the Mentally Ill and Reactions to Mental Health Facilities." Social Science and Medicine 13: 281-290.

Elpers, J. R. 1987. "Are We Legislating Reinstitutionalization?" American Journal of Orthopsychiatry 57: 441-446.

Goffman, Erving. 1961. Asylums. New York: Doubleday.

Gudeman, Jon E., and Miles F. Shore. 1984. "Beyond Institutionalization: A New Class of Facilities for the Mentally Ill." New England Journal of Medicine 311: 832-836.

Hogan, Richard. 1986a. "Community Opposition to Group Homes." Social Science Quarterly 67: 442-449.

———. 1986b. "Gaining Community Support for Group Homes." Community Mental Health Journal 22: 117-126.

Kiesler, Charles A. 1982. "Mental Hospitals and Alternative Care." American Psychologist 37: 349-360.

Rabkin, Judith G. 1974. "Public Attitudes Toward Mental Illnesses: A Review of the Literature." Schizophrenia Bulletin 10: 9.

Rabkin, Judith G., Gregory Muhlin, and Patricia W. Cohen. 1984. "What the Neighbors Think: Community Attitudes Toward Local Psychiatric Facilities." Community Mental Health Journal 20: 304-312.

Segal, Steven B., and Trute, B. 1976. "Census Tract Predictors and Social Integration of Sheltered Care Residents." Social Psychiatry 11: 153-165.

Severy, Lawrence, Starr Silvers,and G. H. Wilmouth. 1987. "Receptivity and Planned Change: Community Attitudes Toward Deinstitutionalization." Journal of Applied Psychology 72: 138-145.

Steadman, Henry. 1981. "Critically Reassessing the Accuracy of Public Perceptions of the Dangerousness of the Mentally Ill." Journal of Health and Social Behaviour 22: 310-316.

Test, Mary Ann. 1981. "Effective Community Treatment of the Chronically Mentally Ill: What is Necessary?" Journal of Social Issues 37: 71-86.

ORAL PRESENTATIONS

Planning and making an oral presentation can be a stressful experience. This can be due to a lack of practice but is more usually a reflection of the speaker's confidence in what she or he is doing. In approaching your oral presentation ask yourself the following questions as a guide to your preparations:

- Is my talk interesting?
- Is it focused?
- Is it pitched at an appropriate level?
- Is it the right length?
- Do I fully understand what I am talking about?

Preparing the Presentation

The following aspects should be considered when preparing a talk or presentation:

- **Form** – do not attempt simply to read an essay aloud, word for word. Your written preparation should be in the form of notes which give your talk structure and shape. Make sure that you can easily follow what you have written. Underline or highlight words and phrases which are particularly important and leave generous margins and indentations. Use your notes as a framework from which to develop points more fully as you speak.
- **Audience** – who will be attending your presentation? How much will they know about your topic? What is likely to be the level of interest? Think about these specific points but also consider the occasion or context. For example, your presentation as a student representative to the social science faculty board is of a different order from your presentation to your seminar or project group – a difference which should influence your approach to content, style and time.
- **Content** – effective presentations tend to make fewer points and in a more expressive way than written papers. If you are preparing a presentation from an essay or report you have previously written, it is impor-

tant to establish the main points before giving your talk. Material which is appropriate in an essay, e.g. multiple references and details of methodology are not at all appropriate in an oral presentation. In your writing , you may have described four studies conducted in four different societies, all of which support the conclusion that occupations dominated by men enjoy higher status than than those dominated by women. In your presentation you might present just one of these studies in some detail. Don't hesitate to select material in this way or worry about having sufficient material for your presentation. It is likely that you will need to elaborate explanations of certain concepts, especially when your audience is unfamiliar with your specialist area.

- **Organisation** – your presentation should be organised logically and in a way which is clear to your audience. It is vital that you first establish what your intentions are and how you intend to proceed. Once you have concluded your main exposition, it is always helpful to summarise what you have attempted to say and to identify one or two questions which your audience might like to follow up. In this way you not only structure your presentation but contribute to the ensuing discussion.

- **Time constraints** – your presentation time will almost certainly be limited. This reinforces the need for a clear outline and it is advisable to have a trial run in order to ensure some compatibility between what you wish to say and the time available. Given a busy schedule such practice is difficult, but will almost certainly be rewarded – even in the absence of an audience! You will become more confident and familiar with your material and gain invaluable experience of timing your presentation.

- **Style** – try to talk in a way which your audience will find accessible and avoid complicated technical language or lengthy, convoluted explanations. The presentation is the occasion for some important points to be made in a memorable way. The ability to communicate ideas in a direct and uncomplicated way is often one measure of a communicator's grasp of a specialist field.

Making the Presentation

Some practical suggestions include:

- Check the room in advance of your presentation. If you plan to use transparencies on an overhead projector make sure that this facility is available and working – and that you know how to use it. Check carefully any other items you plan to use, e.g. flip-board charts, in the same way.
- Like most people you may be a little nervous before your talk. Recognise this and, before starting, establish, in an unhurried way, that everything you need is in place and you are quite ready to begin. Make a conscious effort to speak slowly.
- Be flexible and try to adapt your delivery to the audience's reaction. Watch what they are doing as you speak and offer to expand or clarify a point depending upon what you perceive. It is advisable to have additional examples available which you can introduce if your audience appears to be unclear.
- Emphasise the organisation of your presentation by giving clear verbal 'signposts' of each major point. Change your tone of voice, pause and provide examples to explain particular points. Begin by giving a direct summary statement of your conclusion, followed by an outline of the issues you will be discussing. About two-thirds of the way through, it may be appropriate to indicate that you are approaching the end of your presentation by saying something like, 'I want to devote most of the remaining few minutes to . . .' Avoid using words like 'finally', or 'to conclude', in the middle of your presentation. Your audience may wonder why you are continuing, half an hour later!
- Answering questions will be easier if your preparation has been sound. Try to organise your answer to the question that is being asked; be brief and resist the temptation to launch into another presentation. If you find a question difficult, it is always worth asking for clarification or asking the person to rephrase it. If you still don't know the answer, it is best to say so and ask the questioner how she or he might respond.

ESSAY EXAMINATIONS

In common with other students you probably dislike examinations, but it is possible that at least part of this distaste is related to a misperception of their nature and purpose. Your tutors are not looking for profound and original answers, especially when you are writing under formal examination conditions. Essentially, they wish to see a serious attempt to answer set questions in a logical, well-organised manner that indicates that you have undertaken sufficient reading and have reached an understanding of the major themes and issues which have been discussed during the course.

Preparation

This is greatly helped by working continuously throughout the course. Completing earlier assignments, engaging in the recommended reading and fully participating in your course of study makes preparing for the examinations a lot easier than it otherwise might be. Preparation should be a final stage in a cumulative process, building on the solid foundation of previous work – rather than a disorganised, last-minute endeavour. As you approach your unseen examination paper, consider the following points:

- Go through your previous reading and your written assignments with a view to identifying the main concepts and ideas. Most courses do not rely on one set text so you will need to co-ordinate your understanding across a range of different sources. A comprehensive and well-structured set of notes is invaluable.
- Search for connections between course materials which you have already encountered and with which you are most familiar. Consolidate your knowledge and understanding in these areas, and build upon your own cognitive map of specialist knowledge (see Chapter Two).
- Select, for concentrated preparation, those areas in which you have a special interest. Examinations are not a test of everything that you have studied so it is important to develop a deeper understanding of selected areas of study. However, do not over-specialise. Remember, at undergraduate level you must demonstrate a range and breadth of knowledge.

- You are strongly advised to practise writing under examination conditions, even if this means arranging your own 'mock' examination. Your tutor should be able to provide one or two trial questions. (Preparing for a three-hour examination might involve writing for half this time, say an hour and a half.) You might work on this with one or two other students – this will help simulate examination conditions, while at the same time providing you with assessors to mark and discuss your work. Following this form of practice will help to create confidence for the 'real thing'.

Taking the Examination

When taking an examination within prescribed time limits and under set conditions you should aim to:

- Read through the entire examination paper before writing anything, and clarify with the invigilator any point about which you are unclear. Gaining an overview in this way can help to reduce tension.
- Answer first the questions about which you are most confident. Note any specifications which have been made, for example as regards weighting, or restrictions on answering questions from particular sections. Obviously, it is in your interests to concentrate on the questions that are most significant and important.
- Read through each question carefully and ensure that you answer the question which is before you and not the one you think should have been asked. As in your course work essays, analysis and views substantiated by relevant evidence are more important than lengthy factual or descriptive accounts.
- Take a few minutes to prepare a brief outline for each question you decide to answer. This enables you to select the more important and significant elements for a particular answer, as well as helping you to 'pace' yourself within each answer.
- Organise and manage your time very strictly. You must complete the required number of questions, devoting a reasonable proportion of your time to each.

Sample examination answers

Here are two answers to a question that appeared on a final examination in an Introductory Sociology class. The question was, 'In what ways does Ralph Turner's description of the origins of significant social movements differ from earlier strain theories?' Answering this question requires writing a comparison. The student must first describe 'earlier strain theories' of social movements and then show how Turner's theory differs from these.

There are several important differences (in addition to length) between these two answers. The first answer – the weaker of the two – moves too quickly to a discussion of Turner's work. Although the author need not offer a definition of social movements, she should provide a more detailed description of strain theories. Similarly, when the author of Answer A turns to discussion of Turner's work, she does not provide enough detail about his theory of social movements. Her discussion of redefining the situation as injustice rather than misfortune dominates the remainder of the answer, yet different types of social movements are neither described nor illustrated.

ANSWER A

Clear exposition of strain theories needed

Earlier strain theories stated that whenever the conditions of a certain group of people got bad enough, they would rebel or revolt and try to change and improve their situation. However, this explanation didn't give reasons as to why, when conditions were bad for an extended period of time, people would rebel at one specific time.

Need to be more specific

Turner's description varied from these earlier theories in that he argued that in addition to bad conditions, it was necessary for the people in this situation to redefine their situation, labelling it as no longer tolerable. Generally, Turner explained that this redefinition would come about after an improvement in the people's situation, at which time they would look back and decide that the conditions that they had accepted all along were, in fact, no longer acceptable.

The question of redefining a situation has to do with how the situation is <u>perceived</u>. A classic example of this would be 'misfortune' versus 'fate'. In the former, the situation is defined as being bad, but the victim doesn't blame anyone or seek reparations. The situation is seen as something that can't be helped, perhaps a consequence of fate. In the latter, the situation is also perceived as being bad, but it is no longer 'accepted', in any sense of the word. It is now perceived as someone's (or something's) fault. Here, some sort of reparation or compensation is due the victim.

What about some examples analysed by Turner?

With these cases, the reaction of the victim varied, depending on how the situation is perceived and defined ('misfortune' or 'injustice'). With a misfortune, the victim does not feel necessarily entitled to help or reparation, and as such, his or her only recourse in seeking such assistance would be to beg or plead. When an injustice is done, the victim feels entitled to such help or reparations, and as such, feels free to demand it.

Repeats points from previous paragraph, doesn't add new information

In addition to the problems I have already mentioned, Answer A is somewhat repetitive. The last paragraph does little more than reiterate the issues presented in the previous paragraph.

The second answer, in contrast, begins by defining social movements and summarising earlier strain theories. It then goes on to describe three previous theories, in each case referring to their authors. After an effective transition at the beginning of the third pargraph, the author provides detailed discussion of Turner's theory of social movements. She writes about the critical importance of redefining social conditions in the context of three types of social movement described by Turner, offering examples of each type, and concludes by describing the conditions under which these redefinitions occur.

ANSWER B

Many social scientists have attempted to explain social movements, events that occur when people come together with the intention of bringing about or resisting cultural, economic or political change. Early strain theories assumed that when enough discontent arises among enough people, the inevitable result is an outburst of some kind. Alexis de Tocqueville suggested that a social movement takes place after a period of strain, followed by a period of advancement. Once an oppressed people received a taste of 'the good life', they would no longer be able to suffer silently. Karl Marx argued that when the peasants became so pauperized, starving and poor that they could no longer stand it, they would initiate the Communist Revolution. Building on these theories, James Davis, a contemporary social scientist, claimed that a social movement is likely to occur after a period of advancement, followed by a period of stagnation. Employing the notion of 'increasing expectancies', he argued that people would continue to expect more and that when it never came, they would join together in a social movement.

None of these strain explanations accounts for the fact that social conditions are bad for some people all of the time. Taking Marx's example, the question could be asked: 'Why didn't the peasants, who had been suffering for centuries, rebel sooner?'

Ralph Turner's description of the origins of significant social movements supplies the answer to this question. Turner felt that strain was not enough: oppressed groups must redefine their situation. Where they once saw their conditions as misfortune – as a fate which they could do little to change – they come to see the same condition as

Good succinct definition

Good summary

Relevant examples

Good transition

Important point emphasized

Good transition

an injustice, brought about by others. When the condition is defined as an injustice, the frequent response is revolt.

Detailed information of Turner's theory, coupled with relevant examples

Turner distinguished three types of social movements and the redefinition necessary for them to occur. In a liberal humanitarian movement, such as the French Revolution, people come to see their inability to participate in politics as an injustice. In social reform movements, such as the Communist Revolution, people redefine their lack of material wealth as an injustice. Finally, in contemporary social movements, such as the Women's Liberation Movement, the denial of personal fulfilment is no longer seen as an avoidable misfortune but as curable injustice.

Good extension of ideas raised in previous paragraph

Turner's theory, after answering the question of why revolt takes place when it does, goes on to explain why the redefinition of social conditions occurs. According to Turner, people redefine their condition when there is a rise in the conditions of the major class without a corresponding increase in other social statuses. This inconsistency propels them to act. In a liberal humanitarian movement, a rise in economic wealth, but a lack of political power, can be viewed as the motivating inconsistency. In social reform movements, greater numbers acquiring jobs but not job security can be seen as a cause. The inconsistency that promotes a contemporary reform movement is a rise in personal autonomy, but a social inhibition to exercise this independence.

Although both of these answers make the same general point, the second answer is more thorough and informative. Providing clear definitions and using well-chosen examples, the author of the second answer has written a significantly stronger essay.

5. Research-Based Writing

The dissertation form – or extended essay/report style – involves the presentation of primary (as opposed to secondary) research. In other words, this chapter is about those assignments in which you are involved in collecting and analysing your data from the 'real world'.

Writing an effective research-based assignment involves the transfer and application of the skills described in Chapter Three. For example, you must be able to summarise previous research (as you would in reviewing a book), critically analyse and evaluate pertinent research studies (as in a literature review) and summarise your findings (as you would in abstracting a journal article). All research seeks to answer questions. Consequently, research papers, regardless of their particular form and length, identify a problem, shape this problem into a testable hypothesis and report and analyse the results of such testing.

QUANTITATIVE RESEARCH

Social scientists make a distinction between two broad methodologies used to collect data: **quantitative** and **qualitative** approaches. Quantitative methodologies are useful when the goal of the study is to represent some phenomenon numerically, for example, survey research on smoking habits or attitudes towards drunken driving. Quantitative methods are also used in many other types of research, for example, studies of community crimes rates, aggregate changes in population, immigration figures, etc. The results of quantitative studies are frequently expressed in statistical form; it is on this basis that researchers seek to make inferences about a larger population from which the sample is drawn.

QUALITATIVE RESEARCH

Qualitative methods are best suited to answering questions about social organisation and processes. For example, how does one 'become' a marihuana user (Becker 1963), how do working class 'kids' get working class jobs (Willis 1977)?

Qualitative researchers may, of course, report numerical findings to support these arguments, but they are chiefly concerned with illustrating the richness and expressiveness of social interaction as it occurs within specific contexts. In doing so, they develop topologies or modal categories of social action (for example, different styles of leadership) and they point to the limitations of these categories as revealed by variations among the persons studied.

While philosophical and methodological differences distinguish quantitative and qualitative research, both approaches utilise similar organising principles so that up to a point, it is possible to discuss these together. However, there are major differences in the presentation of research findings and consequently these are discussed separately, later in the chapter.

ORGANISING YOUR RESEARCH REPORT

There is general agreement about the way in which you should organise your report or dissertation and present the findings of your research. The widely accepted pattern is as follows:

- Title page
- Contents
- Abstract

- Introduction; statement of research problem; issues to be considered
- Review of relevant literature
- Methods, design and approach followed
- Findings; statement of results
- Discussion; interpretation, significance and evaluation of results
- Summary of conclusions
- References, i.e. made in the text of your report
- Bibliography (wider, related reading that has been undertaken but not reported)
- Appendices (where appropriate)

This structure should provide you with a useful frame of reference within which to work, although it is important to emphasise that it is only a framework, open to adjustment and modification, not a fixed template to be followed uncritically. You must be prepared to make modifications and to develop a structure appropriate to your subject matter. Additionally, it is unlikely that you will progress in a strict, linear direction; indeed there are good reasons why you should not attempt to do so. Different parts of a dissertation have different functions. For example, the introduction section is largely descriptive; it aims to identify the research problem and provide a clear statement about the purpose of the report. Detailed discussion and lengthy, critical analysis are unnecessary at this stage. These aspects are dealt with later, in the review of the literature for example, where you will need to put your work into context by considering the background reading you have undertaken for your project. Recognising this difference of purpose should help you to break down the writing task into manageable proportions.

THE TITLE

This is usually something that you will leave until your writing has been concluded, although you will, of course, have a clear idea of your research focus from the outset. Good titles are difficult to construct. They tax your skills at summarising. The aim is to prepare an effective title which accurately conveys the thesis of your report, and there are several ways of achieving this. You might, for example, combine interest with substance by following a general title with a more informative subtitle, a device frequently employed in book titles but less so in journal writing. Examples of this are:

- Wayward Puritans: A study in the sociology of deviance.
- Stigma: Notes on the management of spoils identity.
- The Urban Villagers: Group and class in the life of Italian-Americans.

Above all, titles should be informative, giving enough information to convey the general, theoretical focus of the paper as well as the specific variables used in the research. Try to do all this, but in the fewest words possible!

THE ABSTRACT

Writing an abstract is usually required for longer project reports and dissertations. The abstract serves to highlight the main findings and implications of your research and, again, it should not be too long, i.e. no more than 150 words. Extraneous material, such as hypotheses that you failed to test or sources that were only of minor relevance to your thesis, should not be included. Abstracts are normally written last of all, in the third person, and include a brief reference to any sampling procedures and research methods used.

Example:

Fraser, E. J. P. (1994) 'Problems of Gender in University Mathematics', *British Educational Research Journal*, 20, 2, pp. 147-154.

This article presents the findings of a series of surveys on attitude towards mathematics carried out at the University of Edinburgh, as well as the analysis of national data on women's participation and performance in university mathematics. The main goal of the study was to ascertain whether there were gender differences in mathematics students' attitudes and achievement, and to obtain some idea of the scale of such differences. While some results confirmed findings from previous research regarding women's observed tendency to view mathematics more negatively than men, the overall picture showed only weak evidence of important attitudinal gender differences among the students surveyed. In the course of the surveys, several assumptions regarding the interpretation of perceived gender differences had to be examined and re-evaluated in the context of a framework which took into account the meanings of gender and gender-identity development. The national data showed very small gender differences in final degree results, but there was a rather large difference in women's participation rates between the Scottish and English universities.

THE INTRODUCTION

An effective introduction serves two main purposes. Firstly, it contextualises your research within a larger disciplinary framework and signals how you intend your work to be considered, i.e. following a certain theoretical, methodological or empirical tradition. Secondly, the introduction identifies the main focus or research problem with which you are concerned.

Depending upon the form of study in which you are involved, the nature and purpose of your research may be introduced as a hypothesis. Hypotheses are propositions that represent what we expect to observe or discover in the process of investigative research. They are ideas or statements about something which provide the focus for a study, the major concepts or variables which will be examined; usually, they are drawn from either personal observation or the research of other social scientists.

We usually associate hypotheses with deductive methodological approaches, that is with research strategies that use a general principle (stated in the form of an hypothesis) to explain or understand a set of observations. Hypotheses should be constructed so that it is possible to demonstrate if they are false or potentially incorrect. If our observations support our initial hypothesis, we may claim that the hypothesis has validity; if observations contradict our hypothesis, we must seek an alternative formulation.

There are three types of hypotheses: conditional, relational and causal. Conditional hypotheses are propositions that merely assert a state of being (or condition) of someone or something, e.g. London has a high crime rate; the Labour Party has failed to articulate a clear alternative to the Government's economic policy. Although conditional hypotheses may perform the function of motivating an argument or research strategy, they are less useful in social science writing than the other two types of hypotheses.

Relational hypotheses specify relationship between two or more variables or concepts: they claim that as one variable changes, so does another, or that something is less than or more than something else. To put it another way, relational hypotheses assert the correlation between two or more things (e.g. ' Both the number of functional divisions and the age of the firm are highly correlated with organisational size'; 'Length of sentence varies directly with the number of previous convictions of the offender'; 'Women are more likely than men to support equal opportunities legislation').

Causal hypotheses are a subset of relational hypotheses, in that they express a correlation between two or more variables (i.e. when X is present, Y is also present). But in addition to assuming the mutual occurrence of two factors, causal hypotheses go further to assert that one factor is *responsible* for the other (i.e. X causes Y). To confirm that two things are causally related, one must also be able to show that one is antecedent to the other (i.e. X preceded Y in time) and that the relationship between these two things cannot be explained away by some other factor (i.e. X and Y are only related because of their mutual correlation with some other factor, Z). To illustrate, consider the following causal hypothesis: 'Aggressive behaviour among children results from watching violence on television'. In order to substantiate this hypothesis, one would have to show that as exposure to violent television programmes increases, aggressive behaviour increases (i.e. a relationship or *correlation* is established);

that exposure to violent programmes precedes the aggressive behaviour (i.e. the sequence of events or *temporal* aspects are significant) and that the correlation between exposure to violent programmes and aggressive behaviour is not due to some third factor, such as lack of parental supervision. If any of these conditions is questionable, then the causal relationship between television violence and aggressive behaviour is called into question. Because of the rigorous requirements for causality, relational hypotheses are much more prevalent than causal hypotheses in social science research.

Regardless of the form your research hypotheses take, they should be stated clearly and explicitly in the 'introduction', and provide a framework for the presentation and analysis of findings that follow.

Introductions are frequently organised in point-counter point fashion. They begin with a general statement which may focus upon the type of work that has been done or the general findings from this work. For example:

> 'Students of communities have long been concerned with patterns of neighbourhood change.'

The author then takes exception to this view, using it as a foil against which to present the main contention of his/her study. In doing so the author may draw attention to the omission of an important variable in previous research, for example, '. . . but few have been directly concerned with the role of X in this process . . .'.

This type of introduction satisfies the criteria for an interesting opening as well as providing an immediate sense of context and focus. The challenge in following this strategy is, of course, to sustain your argument, to marshal relevant and compelling evidence which supports the direction you wish to take. One useful device is to qualify your initial claims or observations, thereby deflecting potential criticism.

Another way of beginning your study is to place the topic you have identified within a general class of phenomena, describing how you will discuss the topic. This is particularly useful if you are working on a topic on which little research is available. An ethnographic study of an urban neighbourhood, for example, may offer insights concerning general patterns of social organisation. The study, however, may not have been undertaken in response to omissions in previous research. (You may have been given the assignment by your tutor.) If something like this is the case, you need not search for a way to use the point-counterpoint construction. Simply begin with a general statement that provides a context for your main ideas and concerns followed by an outline describing how you intend to proceed.

LITERATURE REVIEW

Literature should be selected for discussion and analysis on the basis of its relevance to your particular hypothesis or research problem.

Even in an extended essay or dissertation, there are limits to the literature which you can utilise and cite. It is obviously important to discuss the major studies which are relevant to your own work, but how do you evaluate the relative significance of published research? One way is to see if the article is frequently cited in the work of others; it is possible to check this by consulting the *Social Science Citation Index* (see Chapter Two). Another way to establish the significance of a study is to note the source of publication. For example, did it appear in a leading journal within a recognised discipline area? If you have difficulties in deciding the status of various journals, or in deciding upon the significance of research, check your course reading list, especially the journal references, to see which are most frequently cited. Go through your required reading and note the references there. In this way you will begin to gain a familiarity with the more important works in your field.

Remember that your research should be guided by its relevance to the work in which you are engaged, which means that you need to be selective and critical in your approach and use of other research.

RESEARCH METHODS

The methods section describes how you approach your work and how you collect data. It should be detailed and include the following elements:

- Describe the sample and indicate the unit of analysis in your study, i.e. individuals, collectives such as families, clubs and businesses, or artefacts such as newspapers, television programmes or court cases.
- Explain why you selected your specific sample from this larger population of people, groups or objects. If you took a random sample, describe the source, i.e. the telephone directory, court registers, voting lists.
- Discuss how you selected the sample from the list – for example, by numbering each case and selecting cases using a table of random numbers; or by beginning with a random start and selecting every tenth case. If you divided your list into two or more groups before sampling, that is, a **stratified sample**, then state your reasons for doing so.
- If you do not, or cannot, use random sampling technique, state your reasons. Generally, randomness in sample selection is more important in quantitative than in qualitative studies. Even when randomness is not essential to the goals of your research, it is a good idea to briefly discuss the **representativeness** of your sample.
- State the total sample size and where relevant, the response rate. Discuss any problems you encountered in selecting the sample, particularly where these influenced the level of participation in the study.
- Describe the sample in terms of characteristics significant to your investigation. If, in a study of community businesses, the age, size and location of firms are important variables, discuss how they characterise the businesses in your sample.
- Discuss the tools used to observe and record data. For example, did you conduct interviews or administer a questionnaire? How were they organised, i.e. face to face, structured, unstructured? How long did it take you to complete a typical interview?
- Describe the observations that you made for a qualitative field study. Did you keep a journal based upon your observations of this group or setting? What kinds of information did you research? If you conducted a content analysis of a set of artefacts, describe what you looked for in each object in the sample and in what form these data were recorded.
- Specify how the major variable in your study is measured, that is, regardless of the particular methodological approaches used. Usually, this will be the variable you are trying to explain or predict, the **dependent variable**. If, for example, you designed a survey to study alienation

in the workplace, you might write, 'An additional index of alienation was constructed from responses to five questions, each measuring one of the dimensions of alienation defined by Seeman (1954): powerlessness; normlessness; meaninglessness; isolation and self-estrangement. A score of five on the index represents the greatest degree of alienation; a score of zero represented the least degree of alienation.

• Describe how you developed a coding scheme if you use open-ended questions to measure a variable, and *remember*, if you rely on a measurement scheme developed by someone else, be sure to acknowledge your debt.

Finally, it is always useful to provide any additional information necessary to ground your research in a specific context. For example, give the date when your research took place, and the details of any aspects of observation studies you carried out, i.e. your role as observer-participant. You should also record any problems you encounter with data collection, even after careful planning. In this way you can anticipate subsequent criticism of your work.

These different methodological issues are presented as examples only. Do not feel that you have to discuss them in this particular order, nor indeed to the same extent. Your discussion must reflect the range of issues which are relevant to your particular research.

Example: Writing About Methodological Issues

To explore such complex patterns of belief and sentiment about cities, 77 adults were interviewed in four communities in northern California: San Franciso, a central city; Hillcrest, an upper-middle-class suburb; Bayside, a working-class suburb; and Valleytown, a rural small town of contemporary America. Each community is not deemed to be typical of all communities of its type. However, this comparative sample of communities facilitates documentation of views toward urban life in different community contexts and, through comparison, a better appreciation of the range of urban views across community forms (Glaser and Strauss 1967).

Households in each community were selected randomly from dwelling lists in two or more theoretically chosen neighbourhoods. Using census tract data and field observation, middle- and working-class neighbourhoods were designated in each community to ensure class diversity within each community type. Given the racial segregation of suburban and small-town communities in northern California, particularly excluding black people, the San Francisco neighbourhoods selected were composed predominantly of white residents. This ensured that urban residents did not differ significantly in minority background from suburban and small-town residents. Households were sent a letter describing the research; up to four call-backs were made to locate residents and this led to slightly more than half of the originally selected households being interviewed.

The interview focused on issues of community belief and sentiment and utilised open and closed questions. The former were designed to ensure considerable spontaneity, complexity, and richness of responses. Interviews typically lasted one hour and fifteen minutes and, with the permission of the respondents, were taped and transcribed for analysis. With respect to beliefs about cities and other forms of community, respondents were asked first to describe the form of community, in which they resided, based on their designation of that community and then to characterise other types of communities. With respect to community preference, respondents were asked to select the type of community in which they would most and least like to live from the following alternatives: city, suburb, small town, farm countryside or wilderness. (Hummon 1986, p. 5-7)

An effective discussion section builds a strong case, either in support of, or in opposition to, these hypotheses and sets the stage for the interpretations of the data you provide at the conclusion of your paper.

Avoid the temptation to describe your research project chronologically ('First, I did this; then, I did this'). Your research results should be organised around the hypothesis you have stated.

FINDINGS/STATEMENT OF RESULTS

This is an important and difficult section to write. It is not unusual, particularly in a major piece of research work, to find that you have generated a large amount of data; this immediately raises a set of questions about the most appropriate way to present your findings. Broadly, your 'text' results represent a **selection** or **summary** of the total data collected, but you must be careful to provide an accurate picture of what you have found. The form in which you present your research findings will be influenced by your methodological orientation. For example, the results of a quantitative study will normally include tables or figures which summarise the statistical data, while the results of a qualitative research project are likely to be organised around typologies or stages in a process that emerges from your observations. Because of this difference in approach, these two types of writing are discussed separately.

PRESENTING QUANTITATIVE DATA

A large amount of quantitative data can be effectively presented in well-constructed tables and figures. How you do this will depend upon the kind of information you collect and the statistical techniques you have used, e.g. frequency distributions, cross tabulations and regression analyses. The following points should be considered:

- Provide sufficient information in your tables so that they make sense to the reader without reference to the text.
- Number tables consecutively and give each an appropriate title which describes the variables that appear as well as the type of data being presented. For example, 'Degree of Financial Satisfaction by Gross Annual Income', (the word 'by' denotes a cross-tabulation, i.e. a table containing the joint frequency distribution of two variables).
- Avoid compiling too many tables, especially those displaying findings that can be more appropriately described in the text. A few well-chosen and carefully constructed tables can provide the basis for a thoughtful and effective project report or dissertation.

- Construct tables in a standard form and use this consistently throughout the report.
- Place each table on a separate page and indicate the source at the bottom of the table.

When writing about tables try to guide the reader through the significant and important points. For example, you might wish to point out trends in the table. As you move across categories of the independent variable, what happens to the dependent variable? What are the modal categories (i.e. the ones with the greatest frequencies) in the table?

You might wish to highlight the more theoretically or empirically interesting findings in the table. Why are some variables in the equation statistically significant and others not? Why are almost all of the observations concentrated in the extreme diagonal corners of the table? It is unnecessary to discuss everything that appears in a table, but you must make sure that the table, as a whole, warrants inclusion in your paper and that you make reference to it in your text.

PRESENTING QUALITATIVE DATA

The analysis of qualitative data focuses on a thorough description of the organisation and varieties of social life. This does not mean that qualitative analyses ignore the frequency with which certain behaviours occur, only that they concentrate more on the subjective meanings of social behaviour that provide such rich and expressive insights. Qualitative methods are appropriately used in many different forms of research, but are most frequently used to:

- Identify the variation in response to a stated phenomenon (e.g. the roles inmates adopt inside prison).
- The stages in a process (e.g. how someone enters a deviant subculture).
- The social organisation of specific groups or settings (e.g. how family structures develop).

Qualitative analysis seeks to reveal patterns – typical ways in which things happen – in complex behavioural settings. When they succeed, they frequently give the reader a sense of having a direct experience and understanding of social life.

Identifying Response Patterns

One way to organise qualitative data is to construct a typology of responses that encompasses all of the observations you have made. This is an inductive approach, arriving at general patterns from the analysis of specific data. For example, Sykes and Matza (1957) were interested in how delinquents justify their deviance in a terms that are not always recognised as legitimate by others. Their research resulted in a typology of five rationalisations that delinquent boys used to 'neutralise' an image of themselves as deviant:

- Denial of responsibility ('I didn't mean it').
- Denial of injury ('I really didn't hurt anybody').
- Denial of the victim ('They had it coming to them').
- Condemnation of the condemners ('Everybody's picking on me').
- Appeal to higher loyalties ('I didn't do it for myself').

This typology provides a unifying framework for describing a number of seemingly disparate responses that delinquents gave to justify their behaviour. Its general usefulness is evident from its extension to descriptions of rationalisations in other settings.

Identifying Stages in a Process

Research papers that focus on processes can often be organised chronologically. In telling your story from beginning to end, you break down what may appear to be a continuous process into critical stages or 'turning points' in this process. You may be interested, for example, in what it means to become a member of a group, leave a community, learn a new skill, or end a marriage. Although everyone's experience will not be the same, your goal is to identify the characteristics of such a process that are shared by most people you observe.

An example of this type of qualitative research is Vaughan's (1986) study of how people make transitions out of intimate relationships. From a large number of in-depth interviews with people at several different stages in this process (which she refers to as 'uncoupling'), Vaughan argues that regardless of whether the couple were married or living together, gay or straight, one can locate pivotal points in the process of 'uncoupling'.

Although her research focused exclusively on intimate relationships, Vaughan's analysis may help us understand how people make other life-course transitions. The general stages in the process of leave-taking she identifies may appear in other situations, for example, when people leave jobs, schools, neighbourhoods, churches or families.

Identifying Social Organisation

How do groups exert control over their members? How do residents define and respond to neighbourhood problems? Qualitative analyses seek answers to questions like these by describing the norms and behaviour that govern life in a particular setting. The goal of this type of research is to expose the interrelationships among people that locate them in some system of organised activity.

In her study of communal organisations, Kanter (1972) was interested in why some utopian communities fail and others succeed. After cataloguing the specific practices of a sample of utopian communities, Kanter classified these practices into six categories of 'commitment mechanisms' that serve either to detach group members from a previous world or to attach them to a new community. The success of a particular utopian experiment was correlated with the group's ability to secure its membership through a number of these commitment mechanisms.

Like the other studies described above, Kanter's analysis is useful because it is a general aspect of group life, in this case commitment. Although her data were drawn from a particular type of group, the typology of commitment mechanisms Kanter constructed from the groups in general could be used in the study of other group settings.

Guidelines for Presenting Qualitative Data

Qualitative data usually consist of either field notes or direct quotations from interviews. In organising this material for presentation, you may find it helpful to:

- **Indent** and single-space long verbatim quotations or field notes. This format will separate your observations from your discussion of them.

- **Provide a context for your observations.** If you are studying the interactions of members in a particular group, give some background information that will prepare your audience for your analysis. You may want to explain why and how the group started, the variation in sex, race, or class in its membership, or its relationship to other groups. If you are writing a paper in which it makes sense to include verbatim quotations, identify the respondents by social characteristics that are significant to your research. For example, if you ask people questions about how they manage neighbourhood disputes, you might want to identify quotations in terms of the person's sex, age, occupation, and length of residence in the neighbourhood. Be careful not to 'over-identify' respondents to the extent that their anonymity is compromised. Do not, for example, identify a quotation by a respondent's street address or specific job title. Place any identifying information in parenthesis at the end of the quotation. For example:

  > I really don't know when I first sensed that there was a
  > problem with the design of the car. It might have been when
  > the product safety supervisor started complaining about the
  > inconsistent results of the road tests. (Male, 45, research
  > engineer, 12 years with the company.)

- **Select the data you wish to present.** Like quantitative papers that are cluttered with tables, *qualitative* papers that are filled with endless field notes or interviews obscure the point of your research. Choose observations for their representativeness: *one person may speak for many, or one event may illustrate many different facets of group interaction.* The text can then serve as a guide to reading your observations (as with quantitative data) by pointing out the major themes they address.

FINDINGS/SUMMARY OF CONCLUSIONS

Given the context of your work, your position as an under--graduate student and the time and resources available, it will be very difficult for you to produce clear-cut 'results' or findings. Your outcomes will tend to be ambiguous and this is to be expected. What is important is for you to give a brief explanation of why things appear as they are and to consider how aspects of the reseach process, the design of your investigation, the sample you constructed and the interview schedule you used, could be modified in order to avoid problems in the future.

- **Significance** – it is important to assess the significance of your work in relationship to the wider context of your subject area. In other words, you must attempt to anticipate the question, 'So what?' In demonstrating your ability to think beyond the immediacy of your data and relating your work to broader, theoretical frameworks, you will demonstrate impressive levels of analysis and reflection – the very qualities that your tutors hope will characterise your work.
- **Development** – having sought to 'answer' some of your research questions, it is useful to consider possible directions for future research. Research reports frequently make suggestions by way of conclusion. For example, they may suggest an alternative methodological approach to study the same phenomenon, the inclusion of additional variables into the analysis, or the study of other settings to consider questions of reliability of data. It is open to you to put forward some of these possibilities.

REFERENCES

All references cited in your writing should be acknowledged at the end of your work under the heading 'References'. Each entry should be placed in alphabetical order, double-spaced and expressed in a standard form which is used consistently. You should establish with your tutors whether there are any particular institutional or course requirements, for example, the inclusion of a bibliography, which acknowledges sources you have consulted but not cited in your text. (Further details on referencing are given in Chapter Six.)

APPENDICES

Any material that will help the reader to understand your research more fully should be attached, for example, measuring instruments such as interview schedules or questionnaires. As far as possible, avoid lengthy appendices.

6. Writing and its Presentation

The context of your essay, the knowledge of your subject or area of study and the theories and ideas which you analyse, all play a decisive part in assessment; your skill and application in these areas is crucially important.

The way in which you present your findings will influence their impact, so it is important that you develop a sound understanding of the technicalities of essay writing, for example, the use of quotations and methods of citation and referencing. The aim of this chapter is to provide you with a sound basis for producing work of high technical quality.

USING QUOTATIONS

Quotations are powerful writing devices reinforcing and contributing to the ideas and meaning of your writing which you seek to convey. However, they should be used sparingly. When they are not, they can detract from your purpose, prompting your reader to skim through the quoted passages in search of the point you are trying to make. Remember, you are **writing an essay, not compiling an anthology**. Before using a quotation consider the following points:

- **Can I summarise or paraphrase these words in valid and concise terms?** If you can then do so, but be sure to acknowledge the source of your summary. Papers composed of endless streams of direct quotations make boring reading. They demonstrate a failure to understand the source materials themselves, as well as a failure to appreciate the reasons for using a quotation in the first place.

- **Am I using too many quotations?** There are no hard and fast rules about this, but when using a quotation the aim is to enhance your text, while at the same time maintaining a balance between your own words and those of others.
- **Is the quotation essential to the point I wish to make?** Do I adequately explain its use? Make certain that *you*, as well as your readers, know why each quotation appears in your essay. The simplest way to achieve this is to introduce the quotation and then refer to it in subsequent discussion.
- **Is this a special case?** Quotations are sometimes used to call attention to a concept or phrase of particular attribution. For example, many classical social science concepts are associated with their creators: Tonnies – 'Gemeinschaft' and 'Gesellshaft'; Cooley – 'looking glass self'; Gans – 'Urban villagers'; Reisman's 'other directedness'. (The quotation marks signify that the concepts are borrowed and that the intention is to attribute the author's meaning to them.)
- **Sometimes a summary won't do.** It might involve more words or a particularly awkward construction to capture the essence of the quotation, i.e. the author's choice of words cannot be improved. Moreover, it may be the case that the quotation is to be used as evidence for a point you will make, e.g. an extract from an interview you have conducted as part of your research. In such instances do not hesitate to quote directly.

Once you have decided upon which quotations to include in your essay, make sure that you present them consistently in an appropriate form. Apply the following rules:

- **Always identify the source of the quotation.** If you are quoting from a textbook state the author, year of publication and page number, for example:

(Plant 1992, p 106); (Commission for Racial Equality 1986, p 18).

If you are quoting from interviews which you have conducted, give appropriate identifying information in parenthesis after the quotation, e.g. (female, 42, office manager).

- **Distinguish between short and long quotations.** If a quotation is four typewriter/word-processed lines or less, incorporate it (double-spaced) into the text as follows:

   In commenting on the role of secrecy in bureaucracy, Weber observes that "bureaucratic administration always tends to be an administration of 'secret sessions': in so far as it can, it hides its knowledge and action from criticism" (Gerth and Mills 1976, p. 233).

- **Quotations that are longer** than four typewriter lines should be indented, single spaced and separated from the text by two blank lines. Quotation marks should not be used. For example:

   The tendency toward secrecy in certain administrative fields follows their material nature: everywhere that the power interests of the domination structure toward the outside are at stake, whether it is an economic competitor of a private enterprise, or a foreign, potentially hostile polity, we find secrecy (Gerth and Mills 1976, p. 233).

- **Quote materials exactly.** Anything placed within quotation marks should be the exact words found in the source. Do not alter anything in a quotation to make it fit into your text. You should retain the original forms of speech punctuation and any points of emphasis. If necessary you should change your text to conform to the quotation, rather than the other way round.

   For example, in the first quotation from Weber, the phrase 'secret sessions' appears in quotation marks in source. Thus, the quotation marks are retained in the text, but as *single*, rather than *double*, quotes. (Single quotation marks are used for quotations within a quotation.) In the second quotation, because the phrase *the outside* appears in italics in the original text, it is underlined in the quotation. If this phrase had not been emphasised in the original, but I wanted to draw attention to it myself, I would have appended the words "my emphasis" to the citation (e.g. Gerth and Mills 1976, p. 233, "my emphasis").

- **You can include mistakes or even racist or sexist remarks** if they are part of essential quotation. In such cases you should follow the inaccurate or politically incorrect statement with the word 'sic' in parentheses. This makes clear your understanding of such material.

- **If it is necessary to alter a quotation,** perhaps by shortening it, signal the omission of any words by using three full stops. Where you wish to alter the original quotation to include it within the text, identify any words you add by placing them in brackets inside the quotation marks.

REFERENCING

You should try to draw upon a wide range of source material in your written work. There are two ways of doing this. Firstly, there is the Harvard Method, which involves stating the author's name and date following a reference in the text (e.g. Williams, 1961). Alternatively, a number can be used. The second aproach uses footnotes, i.e. the reference is given at the foot of the page containing the reference. This latter approach is less practicable and hence less popular and is not recommended.

The Harvard Method, for example, is a manageable and satisfactory way to state a reference within your text and informs your reader of source materials at a glance. It also links directly with your reference or bibliography section – which is organised in alphabetical order according to authors' names. The above text reference should appear in your reference or bibliography section as follows:

Williams, R. (1961) The Long Revolution. London: Chatto and Windus.

The Harvard Method enables you to provide the full details of your source material – the fundamental aim of any referencing system – and is recommended. Once adopted, you should be consistent and use the same standard form throughout your work.

References or Citations Within the Text

As you will have gathered, the main purpose in referencing is to provide evidence of your own understanding of related works in your subject area and to do so accurately. The specific form of text citation may vary slightly depending upon what is being cited, but the following general rules apply:

1. When the author's name is not mentioned in the text it should be included in the reference or citation, along with the date of publication. Page numbers can be helpful in these instances (they are always used when cited material is quoted directly). For example:

    The image if the frontier evolved out of the 'paired but contradictory ideas of nature and civilisation' (Smith 1954, p. 305).
    These results support the information hypothesis (Ritchey 1976), which argues that migrants learn of economic opportunities from established residents.

2. When an author is mentioned in the text, the name is not repeated in the reference but the date (and, if directly quoted, the page number) is given in parenthesis after the author's name. For example:

    Goldman and Dickens (1983, p. 585) define the 'commodification of the rural myth' as the packaging of the images and value system of rural life as if they are contained in the commodity with which they are being associated.

3. When repeated citations to the same reference are made give the date and page number (if appropriate) for the first citation; for later citations list only the page number. This rule is appropriate when the subject of your paper is a detailed analysis of one or two texts. Because it should be obvious to the reader that you are repeatedly quoting the same source, the date of publication is superfluous. For example:

> The assumptions implicit in Karl Marx's later writing are found in his Economic and Philosophical Manuscripts of 1844 (1961). It is there, for example, that we find the clearest outline of his conceptions regarding human nature. Marx (36) writes: . . .

If however, you make repeated references to several works by one author, you must provide complete citations (including both year of publication and page number) for each work, following the form described in rules 1 and 2.

4. For serial citations (i.e., when several sources provide evidence for the same argument), list the authors in alphabetical order, and separate the citations with semicolons. Enclose the multiple citations in parenthesis, as follows:

> Friends and family members may encourage migration by providing information about economic opportunities or social conditions elsewhere (Bieder 1973; Brown et al. 1963; Choldin 1973; Litwak 1960).

5. When a source has two authors, include both last names in the citation. When the source has three or more authors, list all last names on the first citation in the text; thereafter, follow the first author's name with *et al.* (the Latin abbreviation for *et alii*, meaning 'and other people'). The references section, however, includes the last names of all authors for a given source. The examples in rules 2 and 4 illustrate how to cite works of joint authorship.

When you include two or more works written by the same person in the same year, designate them 'a', 'b', and so forth. For example:

Grove (1970a,b) has been one of the most outspoken critics of labelling theory.

When two or more authors have the same last name, identify each in the text by the appropriate initials. For example:

Evidence that both confirms (R.J. Smith, 1983) and disputes (J.K.Smith, 1984) this hypothesis has been uncovered.

When citing unpublished materials, use 'forthcoming' if the material is scheduled for publication. Otherwise, use 'unpublished' after the author's name. For example:

In the recent article, Hummon (forthcoming) summarises the interdisciplinary literature on place identity.

When the source is on a machine-readable data file, note the producer of the file and the date of production, for example:

The data used in this paper are from the General Social Survey (Institute for Social Research 1989).

The List of References or Works Cited

Whether you are preparing an essay, report or dissertation, it is important to include a list of references which you have used and cited in the text of your work. The reference section is placed after the summary or conclusions and before the appendix; it is organised alphabetically according to the author's name. Each text citation that you have used must be included in your references section.

Sometimes, and particularly in connection with longer forms of writing, you will *refer* to other source material but not actually *cite* it. In these circumstances, a separate section headed '**Bibliography**' can be included;

its contents should be organised in the same way as your reference section.

Methods of presenting reference entries vary between different discipline areas, and between different books and journals. Despite this, there are key elements which characterise all entries, as follows:

- Author's name.
- Author's initials or first name.
- Year of publication.
- Title of book or article.
- Place of publication.
- Publisher.

Consider the following examples and note the use of parenthesis, full stops and commas:

> Barthes, Roland 1973 Mythologies London : Paladin
> Roland Barthes, Mythologies.(London: Paladin, 1973)
> Barthes, R. (1973) Mythologies. London: Paladin.

Each entry is correct and hence a choice has to be made in deciding upon the system you will use. Generally, your tutors will advise you about guidelines established for your course or subject area; the main thing to remember is that you must be consistent and accurate. Maintain a uniform approach, don't mix styles, and always check for accuracy.

Books With a Single Author

References to books include the author's name (family name first followed by the given name), the date of publication, the title of the book, the place of publication and the publisher (in this order). For example:

> Rex, J. (1986) Race and Ethnicity. Milton Keynes: Open
> University Press
> Willis, P. (1977) Learning to Labour.Farnborough: Saxon
> House

Books With More Than One Author

If a book has two authors, list it alphabetically by the last name of the first author, for example:

> Berger, P and Luckman, T. (1972) <u>The Social Construction of Reality</u>. Harmondsworth: Peguin

Government Documents

Unless the author's name appears on the report, list the government agency as the author of the document, for example:

> D.E.S. (1988) <u>Education Reform Act: Local Management of Schools Circular 7/88</u>. London: D.E.S.

Works of Corporate Authorship

Sometimes cities, consulting firms, research agencies or other corporate bodies publish reports where no author is named. In such cases cite the organisation as the author, for example:

> British Refugee Council (1989) <u>Refugee Manifesto</u>. London: British Refugee Council.

Edited Collections

If you cite a book with an editor but no author (e.g. an edited collection of papers written by others) the entry should begin with the editor's family name, for example:

> Brock, C. (ed) (1986) <u>The Caribbean in Europe: aspects of the West Indian experience in Britain France and the Netherlands.</u> London: Frank Cass.

An Article in an Edited Book

A single article in an edited volume containing different articles should be listed by the *author* of the article and not the editor, for example:

> Woodhall, M (1991) 'Human capital concepts'; in Esland,
> G. (ed) Education , Training and Employment. Volume 2 The
> Educational Response. Wokingham: Addison Wesley.

An Article in an Academic Journal

> Hewa, S. (1993) 'Sociology and public policy: the debate
> on value-free social science':
>   International Journal of Sociology and Social Policy, 13,
>   (1/2), 64-82.

A Translated Book

Unless you discuss a translation itself, that is, comparing one translation of a work with another, list the book by its author, not by its translator, for example:

> Habermas, J. (1971) Knowledge and Human Interests.
> Translated by Shapino, J.J. Boston: Beacon Press.

An Article in a Popular Magazine

List the article by the author's family name or, if no author is given, list it in your reference section by the title of the article itself or by the second word, if the first word is 'A', 'An' or 'The'. For example:

> Hills, B.(1993) 'Wonderland oh!' The Face, January, 13-15.

An Article in a Newspaper

It may by possible to give a section number; if not the reference follows that from a magazine.

Unpublished Work

If the work is scheduled for publication, substitute the word 'forthcoming' for the date of publication, omitting any references to volume or page numbers. In all other cases, such as a paper written by a tutor or student and circulated within a university department, substitute the word 'unpublished' for the publication date.

Machine Readable Data Files

Begin the citation to a machine-readable data file with the person or persons responsible for collecting the data; if no individuals are identified, cite the institutional producer of the file.

Multiple Citations for a Single Author

If you cite several works written by the same person, arrange them alphabetically by title, and indent as indicated below:

> Baudrillard, J. (1989) America. London: Verso.
>   (1990a)* Cool Memories. London: Verso
>   (1990b)* Seduction. Basingstoke: Macmillan Education.

* where two works occur in the same year, differentiate using (a), (b), etc.

Combining Entries in a Reference Section

When you have compiled and arranged alphabetically the relevant entries to be included in your reference section, they should be typed on a separate page under the title, 'References'. Begin the first line of each entry against the left hand margin and indent all remaining lines of the entry five to eight spaces. Underline the titles of all books, reports, journals and government documents used.

Example: References Section

Aby, Stephen H. (1987) <u>Sociology: A Guide to Reference and Information Sources</u>. Englewood, CO: Libraries Unlimited, Inc.

Barnet, Sylvan, and Marcia Stubbs (1990) <u>Practical Guide to Writing With Additional Readings</u>. Glenview, IL: Scott, Foreman.

Becker, Howard S. (1963) <u>Outsiders: Studies in the Sociology of Deviance</u>. New York: Free Press.

(1986) <u>Writing for Social Scientists</u>. Chicago: University of Chicago Press.

Cuba, Lee J. (1984) <u>Reorientations of Self: Residential Identification in Anchorage, Alaska</u>. Pp. 219-237.

NOTES

The use of notes within the text is governed by one simple rule: if possible avoid it. The rule is based on the assumption that if an idea is important enough to include in an essay, it can (and should) be incorporated into the text. Nevertheless, there are occasions, particularly when you are writing extended essays, reports or dissertations when notes may be necessary, as follows:

• To provide detailed information that would otherwise detract from the main arguments of your discussion. A note of this type might elaborate on an aspect of your research methodology. For example, you might write that the schedule contained several questions designed to measure a respondent's tolerance for residential integration, and append a footnote describing the exact questions that were asked. If, however, you are planning to attach the interview schedule to the paper as an appendix, draw your reader's attention to this appendix with a parenthetical remark in the text, such as '(see Appendix II.)', rather than use a note.

- To supply additional or analogous examples of points raised in the text. For example:

> As Peter E. Drucker recently observed, management has become all-pervasive, penetrating every nook and cranny of social and individual life and turning into **the way** of acting and doing. Under these conditions the truly important problems managers face do not originate outside management and enterprise. They are problems caused by the very success of management itself. (The New Realities, London: Mandarin, 1990p214).Quoted in Bauman, 2.(1992) Intimations of Post Modernity. London: Routledge p92.

- It may be necessary to explain why something has been omitted from the text. For example 'sex and race have been omitted from text discussion, but neither of these variables exerted significant, independent effects on the dependent variable'.

The Format for Notes

Two types of notes are commonly used: footnotes which appear at the bottom of the appropriate page of text, and endnotes, which are placed at the end of the essay or report. If you are using a typewriter, endnotes are easier to write, but the variety of text-writing software beginning to appear makes footnotes equally painless if you are working with a word processor. If you use endnotes, type them, double spaced, on a separate page with the heading, 'Notes', and place them immediately following the last page of your essay or report. Paginate the notes as though they were additional pages of text, that is, if your text ends on page 22, the first page of notes is numbered page 23.

Both footnotes and endnotes are inserted into the text in the same way. They are numbered consecutively throughout the paper, and are usually placed at the end of the relevant sentence. The number of the note is either a superscript number (placed one-half space above the line of text) or enclosed by brackets immediately following the sentence or phrase being noted.

PLAGIARISM

Scholarship is an enterprise founded on trust. Although social science research is designed so that it can be replicated by others, the result of research studies are seldom verified. Because of the time and effort such verification would require, we must assume that both the data and their interpretation are the honest work of the author of the research. Without these assumptions, academic work would have little value or integrity. That is why the organisations that regulate academic life – universities and professional associations – reserve their harshest penalties for those who fabricate research findings or who appropriate the words and ideas of others.

When you present the words or ideas of an author as if they were your own, you are *plagiarising*. Whether you quote directly or summarise in your own words the ideas of someone else, you must acknowledge your debt. You do so by making proper references to source materials along the lines described above.

Claiming the work of others as your own is difficult to get away with. Your tutors are intimately familiar with the published work in their disciplines; acquiring such an in-depth knowledge of research is a major part of their professional responsibilities, and they can usually recognise that what they are reading has appeared elsewhere.

You can guard against unintentional plagiarism by providing unambiguous citations for either direct quotations or summaries of source materials. For example, assume that in the process of researching a paper on societal responses to deviant behaviour, you come across the following conclusion by John Kitsuse:

> In the modern society, the differentiation of deviants from the non-deviant population is increasingly contingent upon circumstances of situation, place, social and personal biography, and the bureaucratically organised activities and agencies of control (Kitsuse 1962, p. 256).

One way of incorporating this conclusion into your paper is to quote it in its entirety, and acknowledge the source as I have done here. Another approach is to retain some of Kitsuse's words, embedded in the context of your own sentence. For example:

> As a proponent of labelling theory, Kitsuse (1962, p. 256) argues that who and what is defined as deviant has more to do with 'circumstances of situation, place, social and personal biography, and the bureaucratically organised activities and agencies of control' than with the behaviour itself.

A third way to use Kitsuse's observation is to paraphrase it using your own words. A good paraphrase presents the ideas in another voice, but does not attempt to follow the same sentence structure or word choice as that of the source material. An acceptable paraphrase of Kitsuse's material might read something like this (note that because direct quotation is not being used, the reference to the page number is omitted):

> Labelling theorists have concluded that who and what are defined as deviant is determined by a host of factors that have little to do with behaviour itself – where and when the act is committed, who is committing it, and who is responding to it (Kitsuse 1962).

Compare this with a bad paraphrase of the same material:

> In contemporary society, distinguishing deviants from non-deviants is more and more determined by characteristics of context, location, societal and individual biography, and the bureaucratic organisation and agencies of social control (Kitsuse 1962).

Here the writer has merely provided synonyms – 'contemporary society' for Kitsuse's 'modern society,' for example. There is no point to this paraphrase. Verbatim quotation of the original sentence is much to be preferred over this mechanical, word-for-word substitution.

The more obvious forms of copying are easily detected and carry severe penalties in most colleges and universities. One area of difficulty, however, is the 'grey area', in which:

> 'a student may not have copied word for word but nevertheless consciously modelled significant parts of their work on that of others, without attributing this material to the rightful author. This too we consider to be plagiarism in so far as it is unfair if, by doing this, some students manage to achieve significantly better marks than those whose work may appear superficially less impressive but which is at least 100% their own.'
>
> (Dept. of Sociology, University of East London)

AVOIDING SEXIST LANGUAGE

Leading professional organisations have adopted codes of conduct designed to eliminate sexist language. For example, the British Psychological Society has stated that it is:

> 'committed both to science and to the fair treatment of individuals and groups... and authors of journal articles are required to avoid writing in a manner that reinforces questionable attitudes and assumptions about people.'
>
> (British Psychological Society, 1987)

It is important to adopt a similiar position with reference to your own writing. Sexist language creates particular problems in social science writing where gender plays a major role in explaining a variety of social phenomena. The use of masculine pronouns to describe a whole range of different roles in society, for example, managers, deviants, leaders, is to imply that either men occupy the majority of these roles or that men and women enact such roles in the same way. These assumptions may be inaccurate, and the continued use of sexist language is an invitation to criticism and analytical difficulties.

There are two categories of language-use problems: those of **designation** and those of **evaluation**. Problems in these areas can be seen both in terms of **ambiguity** and **referent**, i.e. it is unclear whether remarks are being addressed to men, women or both sexes, and in terms of **stereotyping**, where inaccurate biased remarks are attributed on the basis of little or no evidence. An example of the problem of **designation** is as follows:

> Man's search for knowledge has led him into ways of
> learning that bear examination.

This can be rephrased, in the first person, as follows:

> The search for knowledge has led us into ways of learning
> that bear examination.

Alternatively, a plural use and re-writing in two sentences gives another solution:

> People have continually sought knowledge. The search has
> led them into ways of learning that bear examination.

The following is an example of the problem of **evaluation**:

> Subjects were 16 men and 4 women. The women were
> housewives.
>
> (British Psychological Society, 1987)

In the last example, both men and women should be described in parallel, or both descriptions should be omitted. Moreover, the women are defined in terms of sex and marital status – in a way which excludes men. Terminologies used should apply equally, e.g. homemaker.

In your writing you should be careful to write accurately and avoid sexist language which can distort the meaning of your staements. More precise, non-sexist referents are available for use and some selected examples are indicated below:

Sexist	Non -Sexist
the man in the street	people in general
layman	lay person
man-made	synthetic, artificial, manufactured
the rights of man	peoples'/citizens' rights; the rights of the individual
chairman	chairperson, chair
manhours	workhours
the working man	worker; working person
policeman/fireman	police officer; fire-fighter
masterful	domineering; very skilful

(British Sociological Association, 1987)

Much of the older work in social science is characterised by the generic use of 'man'. This presents difficulties for contemporary readers. In your own writing, ensure that you do not place a similiar burden on your readers.

HETEROSEXISM

Against the background of 'an explosion of discourses around sexuality' (Weeks, 1968, p94) it is important to consider the extent to which your work is heterosexist. For example, in discusssions about 'two earner households,' do phrases like 'the young man and his partner' appear? Men do not occur in lesbian households. In discussions about young women and sexuality, is it assumed that becoming 'sexually active' means becoming 'sexually active' with men? Writing in social science carries the responsibility to ensure that heterosexist assumptions are not uncritically reproduced and that appropriate recognition is given to the realities of sexual diversity.

ANTI-RACIST LANGUAGE

We live in a multi-cultural society but one in which there are major problems of racism and racialism. It is incumbent upon us as social scientists to oppose such discrimination and prejudice and one way of achieving this is to ensure that the language we use is appropriate. The following guidelines have been developed by the British Sociological Association and are included here for your consideration:

- **Afro-Caribbean.** In Britian, this is a preferred term often used by black West Indians. It is a term associated with a commitment to anti-racism.
- **Asian.** Refers to people from the Asian subcontinent, often as ethnic minorities in Britian. However, under some circumstances there may be objections of bracketing together a wide variety of different positions within British society. Also, some members of particular ethnic groups may object to being referred to by their 'country of origin' when they have been living for several generations in Britain.
- **Black.** This term is often used to refer to a variety of non-white groups. The term has taken on more political connotations with the rise of black activism in the USA since the 1960s and now its usage implies solidarity against racism. The idea of 'black' has thus been reclaimed as a source of pride and identity. We should, however, be sensitive to many negative connotations relating to the word 'black' in the English Language (black leg, black list etc.) Some Asians in Britain object to the word 'black' being applied to them and some would argue that it also confuses a number of ethnic groups which should be treated separately – Pakistanis, Bangladeshis, Indians and so on. One solution to this is to refer to 'black people', 'black communities' etc. in the plural to imply that there is a variety of such groups. It is also important to be aware that in some contexts – when discussing South Africa, for example – 'black' can also be used in a racist sense.
- **Coloured.** At one time this was considered an acceptable term to use in the USA. However, since the 1990s it has been regarded as offensive to many black people.
- **Classifications.** The Commission for Racial Equality has produced a list of 'ethnic classifications' for the use of employers and others collecting information for the purpose of Equal Opportunities policies, and this is compatible with that used for the 1991 Census. However,

the Commission recognises that no single classification system will be relevant to all contexts. The classification is as follows:

White
Black-Caribbean
Black-African
Black – Other (please specify)
Indian
Pakistani
Bangladeshi
Chinese
Other (please describe)

- **Ethnic.** This refers to cultural groups of various kinds. It is usually used to refer to black communities in regions of mainly white people – such as Polish or Germans – or to other cultural groups such as Scots or people from Yorkshire. To avoid confusion it is best to spell out the relevant ethnic groups explicitly where this is possible. The extent to which classification of different ethnic groups is appropriate depends upon the context. In some London boroughs, for example, it may be more appropriate to distinguish a number of distinct ethnic groups whereas in other areas of Britain this may not be so appropriate. (See also the discussion under 'minorities'.)
- **Ethnocentric.** This means a tendency to perceive the world from the point of view of one's own culture. Ethnocentrism can lead to racism when applied to issues of race.
- **Half-Caste.** A rather dated term which confused caste with race and has racist connotations. Avoid using this term.
- **Host Society.** Not a helpful term in many cases since former in-migrants soon become part of a host society. It also implies a false sense of unity in the 'host' society and conveys a sense of incomers as being somehow alien. It is preferable to talk of a society receiving migrants.
- **Immigrants.** Under some circumstances people could correctly be described as immigrants – if they are in-migrants from one place to another.

- **Indigenous.** Under some circumstances this can be used to describe particular ethnic groups originating and remaining in a particular region. The United Nations uses the idea of 'indigenous groups' to obtain rights for North American Indians, Aborigines and other groups whose situation has suffered from invading colonists. However, in the British context it is not a helpful term since it would be difficult to identify the indigenous British.
- **Minorities.** Some prefer 'ethnic minorities' although others suggest that this implies that the majority are not ethnic as well, hence an alternative suggestion is that of 'minority ethnics', which avoids this problem. When addressing a US audience it is important to take into account the fact that US sociologists use the term not in a numerical sense but in a power sense. This makes it possible to refer to a numerical majority as a minority if they have minimal power.
- **Non-White.** This may be acceptable where one wishes to refer to, say, whites and non-whites. However, continual reference to non-whites could be perceived as racist. With frequent allusion it would therefore be better to use terms like black people, British Asians, etc. since some black groups would rather be identified in their own right than by reference to whites.
- **Primitive.** This has derogatory overtones and implies an ignorance of the nature of many non-industrial peoples. Use 'non-industrial' instead.
- **Race.** Originally associated with social Darwinism and eugenics and therefore highly pejorative. In a biological sense the word is unhelpful since it does not describe the variety of ethic groups which sociologists would normally wish to identify. However, the term has been reclaimed more recently as a way of describing issues of ethnicity in social contexts and is now used in an anti-racist sense. Some have felt that it is necessary to put the word into inverted commas in order to make it clear that these are social distinctions being referred to rather than biological ones and in order to distance themselves from the original meaning of the term.
- **West Indian.** This term used to refer to people from the West Indies, a region which is highly culturally diverse. It has been replaced by 'Afro Caribbean' when referring to people of West Indian extraction.

It is important to ensure that the language of social science which you acquire is free of bias and prejudice. Careful consideration of the above will help but you will need to take a 'deeper' approach, going beyond everyday interpretations of terms such as 'racism' in order to develop and incorporate an anti-racist perspective in your writing.

The issues of sexism, heterosexism and racism provide complex areas of social and political discourse, frequently characterised by contradictions and conflicts. They highlight the need for a critical approach in your research; a need to question views and assumptions and to open these up for scrutiny and explanation.

7. Revising

In the first chapter we emphasised the importance of re-writing; in this last but one chapter we consider more specific and technical forms of revision. The aim is to enhance the quality of your writing.

As we have seen, revising and re-writing are as much a part of the writing process as committing your initial thoughts to paper. When you read an earlier draft remember the importance of objectifying your writing, of distancing yourself and approaching it as an 'outsider'. Above all, allow time to put your draft aside, preferably for a day or so, in order to return to it suitably refreshed and with a more open mind; again, recalling the discussion in Chapter One, allow plenty of time for revision.

Although revising requires a substantial investment of time and effort, it is unnecessary to know all the details of grammatical form to be a good editor. When seeking to improve your work, pause at sentences which 'don't sound right' and try alternative ways of communicating your ideas. Make a serious attempt to listen to yourself, that is to re-read the offending extract with the aim of making it clear and concise. Seeking to improve your writing in this way has been described by Howard Becker (1986) as editing 'by ear', as you literally attempt to make your writing sound better.

CONTENT

Your purpose should be to make each sentence effective and meaningful;

it should be clear to your reader why you have included it. Consider the following examples drawn from students' writing:

> alcoholism is a social problem
> in history people witnessed and practiced punishment for
>   many centuries and people today still exercise it
> during the nineteenth century the industrial revolution caused
>   many economic, social and political changes

These sentences are somewhat empty and contribute little of substance. You may find this type of phrasing in your earlier drafts, but try to ensure that it doesn't survive to final form. When the time comes to revise, be determined to delete those sentences which fail to contribute adequately to your writing.

CLARITY

Will your reader find your writing clear and comprehensible? They should not have to labour on, continually stopping to work out what it was you had in mind when you wrote a particular sentence. As you revise your paper for clarity give careful thought to the following points:

- **Poor word choice** sometimes obscures meaning. Take, for example, the following sentence:

> There is a distinct relationship between the socialisation
> and selection of group members.

To state that there is a 'distinct relationship' between two things doesn't tell us a great deal. By substituting a more precise adjective the sentence can be made clearer, for example:

> There is an inverse relationship between the socialisation
> and selection of group members.

A final revision might go a stage further, i.e. revise the delayed opening ('There is...') and eliminate other unnecessary words:

> The socialisation and selection of group members are inversely related.

- **Weak intensifiers** such as 'very', 'really', 'actually' and 'certainly', should be avoided. Instead choose words which express your thoughts clearly and accurately. Thus, if something is 'very important', why not describe it as 'decisive', 'essential' or 'indispensable'? What is the difference between 'actually being curved' and 'being curved', or between 'really confident' and 'confident'. Such expressions are acceptable in everyday conversation but inappropriate in social science essays.
- **Vague quantitative references** can detract from the clarity of your writing, for example:

> Most respondents agreed that single women should be able to obtain an abortion.

The question that ought to arise when you are revising is, how many are 'most'? A little over half? Three-quarters? Nine-tenths? You can clarify this finding by substituting a more exact figure, or you can explain what you mean. You could state that:

> Three-quarters (75%) of the respondents agreed that single women should be able to obtain an abortion.

In reporting research findings, words such as 'several', 'many', 'most', 'majority', 'few', 'some' and 'minority' should be avoided or explained. Qualitative results are often more effectively presented in tabular form.

- **Poor sentence organisation.** It is important, particularly in longer sentences, to make sure that phrases that go together are placed alongside each other. For example:

Three groups, each with different motives and goals, led demands for . . .

- **Ambiguous use of pronouns** can create misunderstandings and misinterpretations. In an essay on community homes a student wrote:

    Structuring them as closely as possible to a normal home setting has helped the mentally ill to adjust to the environment outside the hospital.

Doubtless the author intended 'them' to refer to 'community homes', but as this sentence is written, she is 'structuring' people (the mentally ill), not buildings. When revising and re-writing, the confusion can be eliminated by the substitution of 'community homes' for 'them'.

In the following example, the use of 'they' leads to similar problems of ambiguity:

    Although roughly equal numbers of men and women work in white-collar occupations, they are more likely to report greater job satisfaction.

Who are happiest at work; is it men or women? When you are revising, make sure that your reader can easily identify who or what you have in mind when you use various pronouns, i.e. 'it', 'they', 'them', 'these', 'those'. It is better to be repetitive than to risk ambiguity.

CONCISENESS

- Your sentences should make the points you intend in the most economical way possible. Consider this sentence from a paper on the origins of the asylum in the United States:

    Definitions of social deviance, as well as ideas as to what the treatment of social deviants should be, differed greatly

between the Americans of the Colonial period and those of
the Jacksonian period, causing the treatment of these people
to change dramatically.

Is the author saying that as ideas about treating deviance changed,
deviants were treated differently? The vague reference to 'these people', at
the end of the sentence, is also troubling. It would be clearer and more
succinct to write:

Definitions of social deviance differed greatly between the
Colonial and Jacksonian Periods, resulting in a major change
in how deviants were treated.

Passive constructions add words and frequently obscure the intended
subject of the sentence. They should, therefore, be edited out. In a passive construction, the subject does not act but is acted upon: for example,
'the respondent was interviewed by the researcher'. This contrasts with
the active form, 'the researcher interviewed the respondent'. Active constructions can make your writing more clear and concise.

Example: Passive Constructions

Consider the following two sentences alongside their possible revisions:

PASSIVE: With regard to sentencing, women criminals are
treated more favourably than their male counterparts.
ACTIVE: The courts give lighter sentences to women than
to men.
PASSIVE: It was for the benefit of the handicapped
children that the law was brought into effect.
ACTIVE: Congress created the law to benefit handicapped
children.

Elaborate phrasing of simple terms is another example of wordiness. This is of particular concern to social scientists, some of whom have
long been criticised for inventing a language to describe everyday life in

complicated terms. Try to write simply (not simplistically) and directly. If you find yourself writing about the 'socialisation process' or 'individual norms', think about what you want to say and the meaning of such terms and eliminate unnecessary phrases.

A final example combines many of the problems we have been considering:

> Now that it has been discussed whether 'mainstream'
> students will have adverse reactions to the integration process
> those who are directly affected by the Act must be considered.

There are at least four ways in which this sentence can be improved through revision. The author is obviously trying to make a transition from one section of the paper to another but she used a passive construction to do so, i.e. 'now that it has been discovered'. Secondly, the vague phrasing of the sentence obscures its meaning. Are 'mainstream' students adversely affected by integration? If they are not (and this is her point) she should say so. Thirdly, the sentence is too 'wordy'; 'integration process' can be reduced to 'integration' and 'those who are directly affected by the Act' is a needlessly complicated synonym for children with special educational needs. Finally, the sentence ends with another passive construction, 'those...must be considered'. We might revise the sentence as follows

> Since integration does not adversely affect pupils in the
> 'mainstream', its effects on pupils with special education
> needs are now analysed.

FAMILIAR EXPRESSIONS

Familiar expressions can be expressive, but risk excessive familiarity which can cloud meanings. Consider what the author of the following sentence has in mind:

- Telephone interviewing is a quick and dirty way to collect survey data.

What does the author mean by 'quick and dirty'? Is she suggesting that telephone interviewing produces less reliable or less valid information than other methods of data collection?

JARGON

Some social science terms have been incorporated into everyday language and, in the process, have lost their precise and intended meanings. When authors of social science papers misuse such terms, their writing suffers. Two of the most frequently misused social science terms appear in the following sentences:

> Due to the **bureaucracy** of the organisation, I was unable to obtain the average age or average length of employment for each group of workers.
> The fieldwork experience left me feeling quite **alienated**.

The word bureaucracy has a specific meaning in the social sciences; it refers to organisations with hierarchical structures of authority in which relationships among members are based on position and in which formal rules dictate how things are done. In the first example, the author uses bureaucracy to mean the ways in which members shift responsibility to others, making it difficult to obtain information (i.e. equivalent to the everyday expression 'red tape'). Without identifying exactly what aspect of bureaucracy created the problem, the statement is ambiguous.

In the second example, it is impossible to decipher the author's intention in describing the experience as 'alienating'. An informed reader might first ask what the writer is alienated from (work, others or self?) and then wonder what dimension of alienation the writer has in mind (powerlessness, meaninglessness, isolation?). In short, concepts such as alienation and bureaucracy have firmly established meanings in the social sciences; to use them casually reveals a lack of understanding of their deeper, technical meanings.

Don't blame society for everything. Too frequently in student writing society is ascribed enormous and indiscriminate powers to shape human behaviour. For example, 'society encourages people to want things they can't afford', 'Society is responsible for our drug problem today', 'Society rewards conforming behaviour'. Although (to paraphrase Emile Durkheim) society is obviously more than the mere sum of its parts, don't fall into the habit of reifying it. Used indiscriminately, 'society' becomes a vehicle for sloppy social science writing (and thinking).

As you re-read a sentence that contains the word 'society', ask yourself: whom or what do I mean by society? Quite often, you can replace society with a more specific subject: 'Advertisements encourage people to want things they can't afford', 'People take drugs to avoid the responsibilities of everyday life'; 'Parents and teachers reward conforming behaviour among children'. By remembering to state your observations concretely, you will become a better analyst of social life – as well as sparing your reader some confusion.

SPELLING

In revising your essay for spelling, it is important to check thoroughly. For this a good dictionary is indispensable – if you don't own one, buy one. The following are recommended:

- **Collins** *English Dictionary*
- **Longman** *Dictionary of the English Language*
- **Oxford** *English Dictionary*

An authoritative source on the technical problems of language and writing is also useful. The definitive work in the field is *Fowler's Modern English Usage*, Fowler, H.W.(1978) Oxford:Oxford University Press. It is very important to check your written work for spelling; your reader may be sympathetic to your difficulty in writing about complex ideas and phenomena, but if your paper reveals basic errors and misspellings you will quickly lose your reader's goodwill. It is impossible to provide a definitive list of words which are commonly mis-spelt, but those indicated below are particularly troublesome:

Incorrect	Correct
arguement	argument
bourgeouis/boureousie	bourgeois/bourgeoisie
bureacracy	bureaucracy
computor	computer
defendent	defendant
definate	definite
develope	develop
devient, devience	deviant, deviance
enviornment	environment
indispensible	indispensable
intergration	integration
questionaire	questionnaire
respondant	respondent
seperate	separate
visa versa	vice versa

GRAMMATICAL ERRORS

A comprehensive discussion of grammatical errors lies outside the scope of this book, but the following are examples of recurring and more persistent problems in students' writing:

• Run-on sentences and comma faults. Run-on sentences result from writing which lacks appropriate punctuation and fails to separate independent clauses. Comma faults occur when you decide that a comma rather than a full stop will correct the problem of writing run-on sentences. Examples of these faults, first in the context of a sentence, and secondly, of a comma fault, are:

  Richardson's (1955) methodology has been challenged however no one has replicated the study.
  Richardson's (1955) methodology has been challenged, however no one has replicated the study.

There are several ways of revising these grammatical errors, for example:

– use a full stop or semicolon after 'challenged'
– use a comma after challenged and a co-ordinating conjunction e.g. yet, 'no-one' etc
– use a sub-ordinate conjunction, making one of the independent clauses sub-ordinate to the other, e.g. 'Although Richardson's (1955) methodology . . .'

• Difficulties can occur in the use of 'that' and 'which'. 'That' is used to introduce a restrictive relative clause in reference to a person, thing or group. For example, 'it was Manjit that told me'. It is incorrect to use 'that' after a preposition, e.g. 'the men with whom I work' (not 'the men *that* I work with). 'Which' can introduce either a restrictive or non-restrictive clause. Compare: 'I broke the finger that/which I type with'.

• Effect/affect are often misused. As a noun, 'effect' means result, for example:

   The interviewer's sex had an effect on the response to the question

As a verb 'effect' means to bring about, for example:

   The interviewer's sex effected a change in response to this question

'Affect' is usually a verb meaning to influence:

   The interviewer's sex affected the response to this question

Sometimes, particularly in psychology writing , 'affect' is used as a general term to describe feeling, emotion or desire. For example:

   The affective states of the organism have their correlates in the autonomic nervous system.

Care should be taken not to confuse the use of, 'that is' (i.e.) with 'for example' (e.g.) Use i.e. when you provide another way of saying something you have written, e.g. to provide an illustration of something you have written. For example:

> We selected respondents using a systematic random sampling technique, i.e. beginning with a random start, every fifth person was selected from a list of all community residents.
>
> Typologies depicting changes in the dominant form of social organisation, e.g. Tonnie's Gemeinschaft and Gesellschaft, Marx's feudal and capitalistic, Maine's status and contract, are an important part of the intellectual tradition of the social sciences.

The list of social theorists in the last example is indicative rather than definitive, hence it is unnecessary to add more names (those of Durkheim, Weber, Cooley and Parsons could have been added). It is also inappropriate to use the abbreviation etc., meaning 'and so on'. Generally, it is advisable to include all that you wish to say rather than to leave your reader with the impression that you have nothing specifically in mind.

- Do remember that data is the plural of datum. You must link the term with a plural verb, for example, 'the data are consistent', 'these data have not been challenged'.

THE BIG PICTURE: REVISING THE ESSAY AS A WHOLE

If you have been successful in following these suggestions for revision, your paper should be full of sentences that are meaningful, clear, concise and free of spelling and grammatical errors.

However, an effective paper is more than a collection of several pages of well-constructed sentences, and in order to benefit from sentence-by-sentence revision, you must think carefully about how these sentences can be used to build strong paragraphs, and in turn, an effective and successful essay or report. Before you hand in your work, you should consider the writing you have completed as a whole and work through the checklist below:

- **Beginnings** – does the introduction accurately and clearly state the focus or main intention of your essay? The first few paragraphs are crucial and your reader will expect to learn, briefly and in an organised way, what is to follow. Try to capture your reader's interest, perhaps by including an interesting example or analogy; remember to identify the major issues you will address.

- **Organisation** – does the essay move in a logical and orderly way from one main point to another? One way to ensure good organisation is to plan carefully and establish an outline for your proposed essay (see Chapter Four).

- **Consistency** – is the tone of your writing consistent? If you begin using formal language do you maintain this approach throughout? Is your choice of verb tense consistent; for example, if you have been describing your research methodology in the past tense, do you present your results using the same tense? Do citations to research materials follow a consistent form?

- **Balance** – what is the balance between description and analysis in your paper? Social science writing relies heavily upon analyses to which you should devote more time, as opposed to descriptive scene setting. Do you have enough evidence to support the points you are making, or do you have too much! In a qualitative analysis based on interview data, for example, two carefully selected quotations from respondents are preferable to large numbers of quotations which simply illustrate the same point. Finally, consider the balance between quotation and summary. Is each quotation necessary and relevant to your analysis? (See Chapters Four and Six on the use of quotations.)

- **Emphasis** – are the major points clearly distinguishable from the minor points? If you are dealing with a lengthy report or long essay or dissertation, it is useful to insert sub-headings or sub-divisions to avoid discursive and irrelevant text (see Chapter Four). However, always check these matters against any course rules and advice you may have been given.

- **Transitions** – does your essay include appropriate transitions, e.g. 'furthermore' . . . 'on the other hand' . . . 'however', as you move from one paragraph to another? Is the purpose of your transition clear, i.e. are you making a point of comparison or contrast? Careful use of transitional words or phrases can help to reduce any uneveness of your writing, and employing comparisons can strengthen the analysis, e.g. 'similarly' . . . 'in addition to' . . . 'moreover', or differences, e.g. 'nonetheless' . . . 'although' . . . 'in contrast'.

Putting it All Together

The following **editor's guide** will be useful as you seek to revise your work effectively and objectively at the end of your writing phase.

First Reading

Is the focus and main purpose of the essay supported by relevant evidence and analysis throughout? On balance, does the paper appear to be well-written, with no obvious weaknesses or omissions? As you complete this first 'edit', write down your impressions, noting any issues or problems which require your attention.

Second Reading

This time consider the following questions as they apply to each paragraph:

- What is the main point? Is it readily identifiable? Is it valid?
- Does the author provide adequate evidence for each argument? Are there adequate details and examples? Do some paragraphs need to be developed or better supported?
- Look specifically for transitional words and phrases (as described above). Do these work? Is the writing still uneven? What changes, additions or deletions are required?

Third Reading

During the third and final reading concentrate on just two characteristics – tone and style. For example, is the writing consistent with the expectations of the reader/audience for whom it is intended? Consider technical aspects of language-use including grammatical constructions, spelling, wordiness and other matters of style, misuse of which can make an essay difficult to read. Indicate which sentences or sections need revision. Revise them.

CONCLUSION

Revising can be time-consuming – and time is a precious commodity. However, managing time for revising and reviewing your work is important and will pay off at the time of assessment.

Overall, you should use this guide flexibly, modifying it to serve your needs. It will be necessary to identify major problems at an early stage so that you have time for rewriting and editing. As you check through your work, try to combine the different elements of editing so that you concentrate on the details of sentence/paragraph construction, while at the same time attending to the total picture. In this way you will not lose overall coherence in the minutiae of particular words and phrases.

8. The Challenge

This short guide has sought to provide practical strategies for improving your writing skills in social science. At one level we have been concerned with a series of technical problems, including how to manage your writing activities and how to carry out effective library research (Chapter Two); how best to plan your writing assignments (Chapter Three) and factors to consider in the presentation of your writing (Chapter Seven). These aspects represent a good foundation upon which you can begin to take control of your own writing and work towards improving its range and quality.

The discussion has had another dimension, concerned with the *process* of writing – for example, writing as drafting, revising and re-writing (Chapter One); the importance of managing and reflecting upon writing (Chapter Two); and approaches to different research methods (Chapter Five). In dealing with these different approaches it is important to acquire deeper motivations; to develop other qualities which will enable you to construct a strong sense of identity within your subject area together with a genuine sense of excellence and enthusiasm for your work. How are these qualities to be developed? To what extent can the challenge of becoming a student in social science be realised?

There are several possibilities. Firstly, you may gain inspiration from the work of a leading theorist or writer-researcher in your field. For example, Professor Mary Evans, reflecting on her experience of the work of C. Wright Mills and his book, *The Power Elite,* observed:

> I read it in 1965 . . . and found it fascinating. The book had a vitality and a verve I did not always find in other required reading. As a second year undergraduate, I did not conceptualise my enthusiasm for Mills as a positive engagement with history, but I did think that this man had written a marvellously vivid study of social power. More important, he wrote it from a particular political position.
>
> (Evans, 1993)

In your work and study try sometimes to look beyond the immediacy and instrumentality of required reading and the next essay – difficult as this can be. Become aware of the styles, perspectives, commitment and ideas of leading theorists in your field of study and, like Professor Evans, you may find a vision and a strength in your subject that you find exciting and sustaining.

Another way of becoming enthused about your subject is an encounter with a memorable and perceptive observation that seems to capture the problem or issue with which you are concerned, in an imaginative, almost poetic way. In a discussion on the problems of the role of the learner and the process of learning, Maxine Greene suggested that:

> . . . the individual, in our case the student, will only be in a position to learn when he (sic) is committed to act upon his world. If he is incapable of breaking with egocentrism, he will remain alienated from himself and his own possibilities; he will wander lost and victimized upon the road; he will be unable to learn.
>
> (Maxine Greene, 1971)

The power of a particular set of words to appeal to individual sensibilities and imaginations is of course variable; the content of what is stated is often less important than the conviction the writing carries, the vision and depth of understanding that it evokes.

Finally, it is important to be contemplative and reflective and to see your studies in a wider context as you seek to extend your own understanding and consolidate your place in your subject area. The main purpose remains:

> . . . among all the details, you will be searching for indicators that might point to the main drift, to the underlying forms and tendencies of the range of society. For in the end, it is this . . . the human variety . . . that you are always writing about. . . .
>
> (Mills, 1970)

Hopefully, you will find inspiration and excitement in your course – a reward for all your hard work and effort. Your challenge is to be open to these possibilities, and to become imaginative and critical in your writing in social science.

APPENDIX I

General Guide to Study Skills

Barnes R. (1992) *Successful Study for Degrees*. London: Routledge.
Well written and analytical approach. Each chapter ends with a check list and action plan. There are good chapters on starting and writing dissertations.

Fairbairn, G.J. and Winch, C. (1991) *Reading, Writing and Reasoning*. Milton Keynes: Open University Press.
A general approach with the main emphasis on the development of successful writing skills.

Northedge, A. (1990) *The Good Study Guide*. Milton Keynes: Open University Press.
A comprehensive treatment of study skills with effective sections on reading and note-taking, learning in groups and learning from the media.

Marshall, L. and Rowland F. (1993) *A Guide to Learning Independently* (Second Edition) Buckingham: Open University Press.
A well-established guide now suitably revised with a clear emphasis on learning strategies for individual students.

Turabian, K.L. (1976) *Students Guide for Writing College Papers* (Third Edition). Chicago: University of Chicago Press.
A classic guide. Authoritative with great technical detail especially grammatical form but note, presentation is from an American perspective.

Guides in Social Science

Becker, H.S. (1986) *Writing for Social Scientists*. London: University of Chicago Press.
Classic, subjective statement from this doyen of American sociology. An interesting read, less a technical guide that a illuminative analysis of some of the problems defined by Becker and his students.

Bell, J. (1993) *Doing your research Project. A Guide for First-Time Researchers in Education and Social Science* (Second Edition). Milton Keynes: Open University Press.
Clear, well-organised guide. Good chapters on planning dissertations.

Dunleavy, P. (1986) *Studying for a Degree in the Humanities and Social Sciences.* Basingstoke: Macmillan.
The book is linked to student progress through an undergraduate pro-gramme of study and contains useful references for the various disciplines in social science including 'think' books for further reading.

Taylor, G. (1989) *The Student Writing Guide for the Arts and Social Sciences.* Cambridge: Cambridge University Press.
Detailed examination of the processes underlying writing skills. A substantial section on language use and analysis is included.

Wright Mills. C. (1970) *The Sociological Imagination.* Harmondsworth: Pelican Books.
An inspiration to us all! The chapter on intellectual craftsmanship is essential reading for would-be social scientists.

Learning Support Guides

University of East London (1992) *Skills For Success.* Barking: University of East London.
A guide for new students with a focus on study and social skills needed, particularly during the first six months of study. A tutor's guide on how to use the pack is also available.

University of Sunderland (1993) *The Effective Learning Programme.* Sun-derland: Learning Development Services.
A comprehensive guide for students in higher education which com-prises six different sections, including becoming a student, collecting and organising information, writing, assessment and working in groups. Based on open-learning methods and produced to a high quality finish.

FURTHER ACKNOWLEDGEMENTS

Excerpt from 'Reorientations of Self: Residential Identification in Anchorage Alaska' by Lee J. Cuba, *Studies in Symbolic Interaction*, Vol. 5, pp. 219-237 (1984). Copyright © 1984 JAI Press Inc. Reprinted with permission of JAI Press Inc.

Student book review. Reprinted by permission of Elizabeth L. Stone.

Book review by Gerald N. Grob of *The Discovery of the Asylum: Social Order and Disorder in the New Republic* by David J. Rothman, *Political Science Quarterly*, Vol. 87: 325-326, 1972. Reprinted with permission of the Department of Political Science, Barnard College, Columbia University.

Excerpt from 'Sex Roles: The Division of Labor at Home and in the Workplace' by Joanne Miller and Howard H. Garrison. Reproduced with permission from the *Annual Reivew of Sociology*, Vol. 8, © 1982 by Annual Reviews Inc.

Excerpt from 'The Dangers of Dependency' by Karl Pillemer. © 1985 by the Society for the Study of Social Problems. Reprinted from *Social Problems*, Vol. 33, No. 2, December 1985, p. 146, by permission.
Excerpt from 'Urban Views: Popular Perspectives on City Life' by David M. Hummon, *Urban Life, A Journal of Ethnographic Research*, Vol. 15, No. 1, April 1986, pp. 4-7. Copyright © 1986 by Sage Publications, Inc. All rights reserved. Reprinted with permission of Sage Publications, Inc.

Maisello, L. (1993) *The Process of Writing*, National Resource College for the Freshman Year Experience, University of South Carolina.

Plagiarism guidelines, Department of Combined Social Sciences, University of East London.

Anti-sexist guidelines, British Psychological Society.

Anti-racist guidelines, British Sociological Association.

Time management guidelines, Learning Development Services, University of Sunderland.

Every effort has been made to contact all copyright holders, but if any have been inadvertently overlooked the publisher would be pleased to hear from them and to make the necessary arrangement at the first opportunity.

Index